T0129943

DIARY OF A BULLIED CHILD: SMELL OF STARDOM

TINA L. CROOM

WestBow
PRESS
A DIVISION OF THOMAS NELSON

WestBow Press books may be ordered through booksellers or by contacting:

WestBow Press
A Division of Thomas Nelson
1663 Liberty Drive
Bloomington, IN 47403
www.westbowpress.com
1-(866) 928-1240

Because of the dynamic nature of the Internet, any web addresses or links contained in this book may have changed since publication and may no longer be valid. The views expressed in this work are solely those of the author and do not necessarily reflect the views of the publisher, and the publisher hereby disclaims any responsibility for them.

Any people depicted in stock imagery provided by Thinkstock are models, and such images are being used for illustrative purposes only.

Certain stock imagery © Thinkstock.

ISBN: 978-1-4497-6640-5 (hc)
ISBN: 978-1-4497-1847-3 (sc)
ISBN: 978-1-4497-1846-6 (e)

Library of Congress Control Number: 2011931147

Printed in the United States of America

WestBow Press rev. date: 10/12/2012

CONTENTS

PART 1

MY STORY AND THE AFTERMATH

INTRODUCTION

I am writing this book to be an inspiration to others, to share my success about bullying, and hopefully to change someone else's life. Bullying in our schools is a serious issue that must be dealt with wholeheartedly. From parents, children, teachers, and principles to superintendents, let's work together and reduce suicide rates, dropout rates, and violence in schools. If we tackle this problem today and implement anti-bullying policies in all states, we would send a powerful message and stop bullies dead in their tracks before they attack innocent victims. Today can be a start to a new beginning, and tomorrow there will be more kids graduating and becoming the leaders for our future.

Bullying is one of the main causes of our high failure rates in most schools. Our children are afraid to go to the bus stop, to the library to study, to the classroom to learn, or to the activity center where they interact with their peers. They are literally terrified that attacks will be made mentally, verbally, or physically.

To the parents, let's start showing our kids more affection, love, attention, and sense of belonging and provide a stable home environment because bullies look for other ways of getting attention when these elements are lacking. It starts at home. Whether your child is a bully, gets bullied, or is at risk of suicide is solely at your discretion. How you handle your situation at home could result in saving another child's life. Don't let someone else's child be a victim of your failures. If you are having problems with a significant other or spouse, don't allow your children to witness such negative behavior. Your child will act out those behaviors because that's all they witness. They are not exercising positive characteristics because of negative environments.

To the children that are bullied, get to know yourselves. Let's build self-esteem so that if a bully throws physical, mental, or verbal threats your way, you will be proactive rather than reactive. What I mean by this is if someone walks up to you and calls you ugly, you will be proactive by responding, "I looked in the mirror today and saw beauty," and walking away with a smile. Be careful how you react, because the bully can gain control over your mind if they see you cry or weakened from the bullet that they have thrown. They feel whatever they say; if you believe it, they can use that against you during the duration of the school year. Allow yourself some time every day to go over your strengths and weaknesses. Be prepared for the worst-case scenario. I survived bullying because I was proactive and was ready at any given time. I never cried because my self-esteem didn't allow me to believe what the bullies were saying. I knew I wasn't as pretty as most young girls, but I wasn't bad-looking either. Being honest with yourself and knowing that you are a "work in progress" are key. You need to walk with pride, hold your head high, and know that God is on your side. Go to school, focus on bettering yourself, keep your grades up, and achieve academic success from grammar school to college. Block out any negativity because it will detour you from the road to success. The aftermath of being bullied can be either a disaster or a happily-ever-after, as it was for me.

Most distant relatives in my family underestimated my intelligence and my gifts because all they saw was the bullied Tina who was in all the fights in school. One of my distant cousins said to me, "I thought you were going to be a high school dropout." I surprised my whole family when I was the first to get my bachelor's degree from college. Challenge yourself today by striving to be the best you can be and prove to everyone that yours won't be a story linked to failure. You hold the key to your future and the power to make the decision to never give up on your life. Become a survivor of bullying and never look back.

To the bullies, let's seek ways to better our character and social environment. If you are lashing out at others because you lack the proper motivation and love in your home, discuss this with your parents. You play a key role in making your situation more functional. Your parents should know your inner thoughts and their connection with your unhappiness. Our schools are supposed to be the place we can call our "home away from home." Your actions pose a threat to this for others, and if you don't feel comfortable talking to your parents because they are the problem, then feel free to discuss your issues with the school counselor. If you choose to keep your problems within, it will make the problems grow and cause our precious kids to commit suicide or bring violence into our schools by carrying in guns and weapons to protect themselves from people like you. The tables can then turn, and you can become a victim of your own crime. You can be the one on the receiving end of the bullet. Bullies like you feel the only way to get attention from your peers is to "de-grade" someone to "up-grade" your own name. Stop worrying about what others think and go to school for educational purposes. If your classmates don't accept you because of the way you look, walk, or talk or because of the clothes and shoes you wear, or whatever the case may be, God accepts you as-is. You have a friend that is constant and will never judge you for materialistic things. If your main focus for going to school is to hurt another innocent child or to get initiated into gang violence, that will lead you to prison or to the road to failure. Choose the road to improvement and change your evil ways. Stop harassing kids and become more noticed for doing good deeds and having a bright future ahead.

It hurts my heart and troubles my spirit to turn on the television and see that numerous kids today are committing suicide because they can't deal with bullying. I am going to do everything in my power to make the message very clear: no more bullying. The bullies started attacking me in 1990 and now, twenty years later, the "aftermath," God has blessed me to share my story and empower minds all over the world. One day soon, our kids will enjoy going to school and paying attention in class, be motivated to achieve success, have the brains to help another student that is distracted by bullies, and have the teacher/student interaction that helps strengthen their foundation of knowledge.

God wants me to relive my bullying devastations so that each bullied child will know that if I survived the pain, horror, and torment, then so can you. We all have different reasons why we are attacked, but the message is the same: never give up on your life! Regardless of what the bullies think of you, we are made beautiful and equal in the eyes of the Lord. Hold on to his unchanging hand and know that you are chosen one day to share your survival story!

CHAPTER 1
FAMILY OF STARS

As a little girl, I was one of seven kids born and raised in a small town named Covington, Tennessee. During my childhood, we experienced unlimited playtime, playing kickball for competition and street racing all night, but during the school week our parents would be stricter, so we would be able to complete our schooling for the year on time. They stressed to us that if you didn't do your preparation throughout the year, you would be considered a failure at grading time.

We would have family time with the grandparents, staying over all night and eating Grandmother's good cooking. She would cook breakfast for us in the morning, lunch (good ol' hamburgers made with crackers and eggs), and dinner at night. There was something about Granny's cooking. My siblings and I looked forward to it. She would bake a cake that tasted so different from other bakers'. Everybody in Covington loved my grandmother's cooking and baking. She was not only gifted in the kitchen, but she also had the gift of prophecy and was a florist and retired teacher. My grandfather was more of a supporting figure in her life because he recognized her leadership abilities. They would make a great drama scene because she was the talkative and inspirational one, and he always told her argumentatively, "Lucille, why don't you shut up?" She couldn't shut up because it was God's destiny to evolve her through her voice to teach and drive the success of her family. Added to the gift of prophecy, she was gifted to have talent as a successful business owner. Her business was named Croom's Wedding and Flower Shop. She provided wedding and floral service to many customers in Covington and its surrounding areas. Everything she touched turned to gold.

My grandparents were married for over fifty years and had one child. His name was Jerry Croom III, my father. He then had seven children with Allison, my mother, and their names were Kelly, Michelle, John, Princess P, Richard, Tina, and Joe. When I distinguish the roles of my parents, you will notice that they are reversed because my dad was the strong force driving the success of his family. Their roles were different because Mom would be present, but speechless, just like Grandfather. She told Dad all the time to be quiet, that you don't have to discuss everything on your mind.

It was divine intervention in my parents' life to have a total of seven kids. We were each other's best friends. It was an exciting experience to come home from school each and every day. I have discovered that each member of the family tree plays a key role in your life's journey. Through the genes of parents, each and every child will be somewhat different in their own unique way. Kelly was always a loner. She took after mother in a sense because of her anti-social tendencies. We, as sisters and brothers, had different events that we looked forward to each week. As the other siblings gathered after school on Thursdays for *A Different World* (the sitcom series), we would find Kelly in her room all alone looking at TV. I used to tell her, "Kelly, come watch it in the front room with the rest of us," which shows family bonding and interaction. During her adolescent years, she was faced with an esteem crisis. She faced numerous difficulties because of it. Kelly had given up on life, but God felt her life's plan hadn't been fulfilled. She needed an esteem builder that could boost her inner self. Looking for love in all the wrong places, depression was her dilemma. I used to tell her that she was too beautiful to be going through these challenges, not knowing that her temple was incomplete on the inside. This was a journey she had to experience. You have to overcome these obstacles/failures by building up yourself to love yourself. She is now a nurse and has been married to Jay, the love of her life, since 2004. They have a love story of sixteen years, but no kids together. She has a daughter, Desiree from a previous relationship. Kelly couldn't have any more kids, although Jay wanted a couple of little boys.

Michelle was mentally challenged and experienced life way behind her other siblings and peers. During my childhood, our personalities clashed often. We would argue over simple questions that I would ask her. She would chase me because I would ask her, "Why are you eating all the food up?" and she took that very offensively. One day, it all caught up with me. I was admitted to the hospital and had to get stitches in my left hand. It was late one Friday, mom went grocery shopping prior in the week, and when I go to the refridgerator, all the bologna was gone. I knew she ate it up, so confronting her wasn't the right choice but I thought I had a voice. The other siblings was always scared to approach her but I wasn't. It was seven of us, so our parents trying to feed a family, was a task alone. Nonetheless, you don't need one child eating up the food before we get home from school. As we grew older, we were like the best of friends. She had the personality of "I am a great person to be around as long as you don't push my buttons the wrong way." She has two girls, Bessie, and Titania.

John was a sibling who never felt that he got the love, direction, or attention from our parents that he needed. During his adolescent stage, he would find a reason not to be at home. I always thought he sought affection from other parents when he should have communicated his feelings to his own parents, so that they can make life more normal. He felt their attention was not where it needed to be. Not only was dad out catting around and producing two kids on the outside of the marriage, but my brother also thought our parents had their "favorite children." He was under the assumption, Princess P and Richard were the favorites. John barely graduated from high school and, when you don't have drive and ambition, you will be a failure. I wondered why he didn't pursue his talents to become an artist. That is a gift from God, but he doesn't believe in God. The Lord only gave him a glimpse of what his talent was, but disbelieve and the talent will be taken away. He is currently thirty-six and has no stable work history. He did find Tammy, though, the love of his life and has one son, Fred.

Princess P was always a star in every aspect of her life. She is a true model, not only in inner beauty, but in judgment, decision making, and humorous behavior. We share a lot of common values in life. Our personalities match and compliment each other in a God-given way. She is two years apart in age, but closer in the mindset of self-love and self-esteem. A model isn't someone who just runs down the runway, but she is someone who has self-worth and leadership abilities that others can look up to and follow in her footsteps. Princess P found her Mr. Right in ninth grade but left him later in life for six months because he hadn't married her yet. He didn't feel the need to marry when he had the full-course meals and the desserts. Martin would sleep with other women when he already had the one God called for his life. So, Princess P left him to be with another man, Nate, in Nashville, taking her son Danny along, too. Martin awoke me the day I returned back to Rust College for my senior year asking, "Where is Princess P? I haven't seen her in days and something's not adding up." I didn't reveal her location because the Spirit told me to tell him, "If you really love her, then you should marry her." So, she returned and they later wed and have been married for ten years now with two children, Danny and Celise. I really feel that it was the Lord's intervention through my voice that led Martin to marry her at that time. See, the Lord has a way of using his people to step in as he would to make your journey complete.

Richard was a true man indeed. He was the male figure when Dad wasn't around. I truly feel he was called upon to be my hero during my childhood and adolescent years. He would often defend me through fighting other little boys or arguing in fights I was involved in. We were a year apart in age and when I went to high school my freshman year, he was so protective of me. Also, during this time, I always wondered why Princess P and Richard wouldn't include me in any of their photo shoots. They would take pictures together 90 percent of the time whenever portrait studios came to take photos. Was I not pretty enough to make the trio complete? I was a freshman, Richard a sophomore, and Princess P a junior. The same thing would repeat itself over during Princess P's senior year. It didn't really bother me because I wasn't desperate for attention, but I knew one day my question would be answered. He had to transition to college and later found the love of his life, Catherine. They have two girls, Rita and Alicia.

Joe was the miracle child of the family. When he was born, his heart stopped and revived itself all over again. He was always the shyest among the siblings. For him to speak on a topic of conversation it had to be relevant or meaningful. As he grew older, his destination, the bus of entertainment—getting high on marijuana and partaking in sexual activities with numerous women—didn't come to a complete stop. I would often wonder how long he was going to ride, but he said it has taken a little longer than he anticipated. Well, I am hoping it comes to at least a yellow sign soon because the devil will try to destroy you with incurable diseases. So, Joe is living life and attending college in the field of psychology, but is still looking for that sense of purpose.

Last but not least, I was a different human being that always had this drive no one else had. Although my siblings and I share some traits, the trait of ambition was not common. This character trait is common in a child of destiny. This child was born with superiority and her life will be magnified through his glory. I faced a lot of challenges in the outer beauty category, but it was a part of his plan to one day beautify my personal appearance to get me ready for a stage higher than life itself. He would later reveal to me my true calling and purpose in life.

I lived a Holy Ghost-filled life in grammar school until the devil distracted me with temptation, and I admit that I had once backslide. Oftentimes I was bullied for no apparent reason and people wondered how I made it through without having suicidal thoughts like other kids normally would have.

CHAPTER 2
SCARFACE

During my adolescence, my outer glow wasn't as pretty as most young girls. Oftentimes, my mother would put jheri curls in Princess P's and my hair. It would make us look like little tomboys with Adam's apples. I would have little boys bulling me more so than Princess P because her skin was more perfect than mine. Through the inheritance of my mother's side, I would have dark circles around my eyes. They would call me Scarface. With the constant bullying, I never cried. Most of my classmates would have developed low self-esteem due to the root of this evil.

I had a body that was fine as wine, so the bullies targeted the imperfections of my face. We are all created in likeness of him but must know, we are not made perfect. Not only is Jesus the perfect child of his generation, but the greatest of them all. He was the only perfect person to have ever existed. So, in his King James voice, he states, "Many are called but only few are chosen." He demonstrated that those who are chosen will be created with some imperfections. Princess P only had one imperfection and it was that she was born in the garden of Eden with an Adam's apple. My two imperfections were that I was also born with an Adam's apple, but with an "unpretty" face (in the bullies' eyes) that created tension in my childhood as Scarface.

The bullying started in 1990, when I was in the fifth grade. I would find myself fighting with little boys because they were bullying me with name-calling and trying to harm my self-pride. I won the physical fights against little girls. God put me through the test of time when I had to fight against "man" kind. Although the battle was won with one, the next one would be tougher and tougher. My brother Richard would face the impossible. This experience would especially become more overwhelming to him during times when some of the little boys would start to become more attracted to me and start feeling on my booty. Others would call me bad, ugly names. He was just caught in the middle one way or the other. He was frantic and started to fight my battles sometimes because of the sexual tension that he was not pleased with. He didn't want anyone looking at his little sister in such a way.

During fifth grade, some of the little boys created another name for me—"T.I.N.A." T is for Termite, I is for In the face, N is for Naturally ugly, A is for All the time. This was a song that they actually sang. It represented the external bruises and scars that I went through during childhood defending my battles. Although some thought I was cute with a little shape, others always saw the external bruises from all the fights.

In between classes, sometimes I would dodge the bullets by going all around the school to get to my classes. I imagined that they were standing at the lockers, waiting to sing the "ugly" song about me. Some would call it running from the boys, but others would see it as a student trying to focus on the purpose of attending school, and that is to learn. One day, a boy named Mark said, "Where you going, Tina? You can't hide from us." I told him, "I am not hiding. Just trying to get to class." Before I could get the last word out, here came three of his other friends. All of them had a part to the song and showed that it was well-rehearsed. They dramatically sang the four parts to the song. I felt like I died and came back to life.

God was driving my vehicle during the whole disaster in the bullying lane. I spoke with him during this journey and asked him, "Why me?" The little boys didn't seem to stop, and finally it would bother me so much it affected my grades. During that year, my reading teacher told me I would have to attend summer school in order to pass on to the next grade because I failed reading. The road to concentration took a small detour, but I later found it on destiny's highway and never looked back.

Once, in the sixth grade, I remember heading to the bus stop. As I walked up the bus stairs, I looked at the driver and greeted her with a hello. Many of the girls who always picked on me were sitting way at the back of the bus. They saw me stop at the front seat to avoid drama. So here came Wanda. She stepped up to me and asked, "Hey Tina, who hit you in the eye?" I said, "No one hit me in my eye. Why do you ask?" She said in a joking way, to make everybody on the bus laugh, "I asked because it looks like someone hit you in both your eyes." I immediately hit her in the face, and then she hit me with a bat. I took the bat from her and whooped her tail.

One day during my seventh-grade year, I got into another fight because a guy named Stephen had called me ugly. He hit me in the eye and it was swollen for several days. With the ambition and the drive that was instilled from within, I was able to still get up and go to school with a swollen black eye and busted nose. Although my goal was to have perfect attendance in school, I would still miss days because I was a "child of destiny" with "imperfections." The only way I wouldn't go to school is if I was really sick or down. Close friends would wonder why I would show up at school the day after a fight with a black eye and swollen nose. What was important at the time was focusing on the task at hand, to finish school and complete my grammar school education. I never liked to be a day behind on any assignment. My teachers didn't send me home because they knew I had the drive and ambition for school. I knew that would be the foundation of my knowledge.

These acts of bullying continued all the way through high school with this group of guys. Unfortunately, we were all in the same grade. I used to play on the basketball team for the Chargers and we were on our way back from a road game in Brownsville once and Mark along with two others started singing the song about me again. Most players were asleep, but woke up with a chant against Tina. They started laughing at me and I finally struck back and said, "While you all are talking about me, you should look in the mirror at yourselves." Mark wasn't attractive and had fifty-two teeth in the front of his mouth. The other guy, Brian, was dark-skinned with pink, dried-up lips. It looked as if he had girly lipstick on. After this day, there was a little back and forth, but for the most part, the bullying came to a silent close.

Nowadays, kids are being bullied every day at school. Since I was bullied all through grammar school and part of high school, was my calling to be an inspirational advocate for children today? Let my voice be heard through these devastating moments. I am here to tell you, this ride is going to be a gateway to hell if you don't have God on your side. While Mark and his friends would call me out of my name, I would often say to myself, "One day his dirty deed will show his real purpose for picking on me." He could never get a girlfriend, as far as I knew, in grammar school. Didn't anyone want him because he was so ugly? So, while he was making songs for me, he should have been focused on getting himself together—and others would agree, "Let's make some dental appointments." His parents' primary focus should have been not only the personal appearance of their son's mouth, but how he was trying to hurt innocent children with his words at school.

Students in today's society should challenge the person bullying them. If they throw sticks and stones at you, they are trying to keep another peer from throwing at them. I have learned that with being bullied, your bullies have more imperfections than you. I didn't show any emotion because I had high self-esteem, self-love, self-confidence, and a shield of God. Although I didn't shed tears or tell my parents, I felt the pain on the inside. I didn't want my parents to get worked up for nothing. I told myself, "I can get through this because I know I am not what they portray me to be."

The guys obviously had low self-esteem, the reason they picked me to unleash their problems on. Watch very closely and study the person. I think I got under their skin because a lot of times I would just laugh back at them and find faults in their characters. I took mental notes because I didn't have time to stand out at lockers and play their games.

In school, my motivation was to get excellent grades and successfully move onto the next grade. I wasn't satisfied with making Bs and Cs. If it wasn't an A- or higher, that's when it felt like I was a failure. Teachers would say, "She is a perfectionist." All through grammar school and high school, I maintained honor roll status except for the first year the bullying started because I wasn't mentally sure of what was about to happen. God has to intervene and take over your mind, mentally and spiritually.

I used to ponder many days and nights about why was I a target in school. Was it because you have what they want, or is it the way you look, the way you walk with honor roll status, popular in others' eyes, and they are not? Is it due to your positive home atmosphere with both parents, new clothes most of the time, and shoes not worn out? This could be why you may appear to be an easier target to help build their self-worth.

I heard a story on CNN that a kid committed suicide from being bullied. Although I never thought of suicide, I can imagine the pain the child felt. I continued to pray for the family. We need to gain control of what is happening in our school systems. Sometimes bullying can make you stronger, like in my case, and some need guidance on how to handle the situation right at that moment. You can actually walk away a better person. Ask God, "Why me?" He could be testing your faith or trying to see if you are listening to his voice through this trial. See, God tested me through the process and I passed the test of childhood bullying. In life, he will throw many trials before you, but you must know that this is a mental test so that you can provide a "test-imony!"

CHAPTER 3

THE PLAYER'S CLUB

I was introduced early to the Player's Club, at the end of the eighth grade. This place would be the location where the grown and sexy people would hang out. It would be magnificent in a way, where all eyes would be glued to me when I walked in the door. Not forgetting I was Scarface and Termite. Now, all of sudden, the attention would be focused on me in a matter of seconds. Princess P (in the tenth grade) wanted to go to the club, so we went and had a really good time. I received a lot of attention from partygoers. It would be as if no one else was in existence. By this time, I had slowly been transformed into the "destiny child." He knew once the physical attraction started to glow, he was shaping me for who I was becoming, slowly but surely.

Regardless of the name-calling from some of the guys, I always had fun from childhood to adolescent years. My parents would let us go out and enjoy ourselves, but most importantly trusted that we would not allow ourselves to be in reach of any harm. So, we would go to Denim & Diamond, where there was unlimited amount of socialization. The interaction with men was spectacular. Stressing this fact again, I really started to get a lot of attention. The djs from local radio stations would call me out on the air and say "Steroid Booty," which I thought was really funny. I was receiving a lot of compliments like cutie, sexy, hot, or amazing eyes. I heard that saying frequently. Everyone was looking at me with a stare and maybe they started seeing the look of a "young diva." It was somewhat flattering in a sense that I started to feel my inner self was about to change.

So later on, we started to hit up different parties in Memphis, Brownsville, Ripley, and Covington. Princess P and I had other family going with us, but all eyes were on us. We were very popular but he called on me to lead the way from there on out.

CHAPTER 4

THE HYPNOTIZE AND INNER BEAUTY GLOW

I realized at this point in my life that people were fascinated with my inner beauty and glow. God has instilled this in my mind, body, and soul. Since day one, it was developed and blossomed later in life externally. Everywhere I go, whether to the grocery store, mall, or fast food restaurants, and from people of all walks of life, I really never knew the reason why I would get so much attention until he revealed that the inner beauty was filtering its way through my outer self.

People would stop me in public places, telling me their life stories and only have known me for a matter of seconds. So, with that revelation revealed, he told me to start talking back to these people as if I knew them for a lifetime. Their concerns were things in life such as church, family, and relationship problems, and being faced with unlimited amounts of debt. Let's not forget, I was only a teenager, but my maturity level was like that of an adult.

God said that those that are chosen, everything they encounter and touch will be blessed thorough his mercy and glory. These people were hypnotized by my presence and I would note that in my mental diary. The Lord was revealing to me my real purpose in life and he allowed my light to shine so bright that others would be able to see. He wouldn't reveal my whole diary until I was able to handle a glimpse of what was about to be discovered.

I used to work at KFC and Hardee's, and the women I worked with named Sue, Rebecca, Rochelle, and Vicky would get jealous of all the attention I got from male customers. The men use to leave me tips, compliments, and plenty of conversation. They would tell me I was so beautiful and that they would like for me to be their girl. I was flattered by the attention and would walk away with a smile.

The co-workers would roll their eyes, but I told them I didn't care because it wasn't like I was trying to steal all the attention; it would just come naturally. The women said that the men were only trying to talk to me because of my shape, but the first thing the men used to say when first looking at me was, "You have some amazing eyes."

Through my eyes came this astonishing glow of God's love, covering me with life's umbrella. When you awaken, you feel his presence; that's unbelievable to those without a higher power. People would always say, "There something amazing about her." When you walk in a dark room, the lights will suddenly appear on. You will capture the attention of them all, but you will never take the credit. It is the Almighty Lord of Lords!

CHAPTER 5
THE TURNING POINT

During my junior year, 1996, at Covington High School, I had experienced a mental chemical imbalance (how doctors described it) such that my family members and friends thought I was going crazy and losing my mind. Just out of nowhere, I started having visions of famous people such as Tina Turner and the female R & B group called TLC.

I would walk up and down the streets of Covington as if I was famous and the whole world was watching. Everyone had shades on except for me. I told my family, "It appears people are laughing at me." When I got back home, I would tell my sisters, Kelly and Princess P, "Let's go on stage and perform," as if we were a singing sensation and I was the leader. They didn't know how to react.

Also, included among my other visions was that I was getting married to my high school sweetheart, Joseph. I never knew what those visions meant until he started revealing more substance. He was showing me, I was going to be a big name one day, like "Tina" Turner and I was "TLC," Tina LaDawn Croom that I was getting married one day.

Covington is where my garden of Eden all began. Where my grandparents produced one child, then my parents would have seven children. Of those children, one of them was chosen to be God's revelation.

It was strange how, through my mental breakdown, I told my father, Jerry, to drive me out to Joseph's place and ask him if he was about to marry me. Joseph stated, "Mr. Jerry, what are you talking about?" Dad replied back, "Tina said you all are getting married today." With a dumbfounded look, Joseph said, "No, we are not getting married." Dad and I finally left. It was all a part of my journey.

I started my junior year late because I had been in Charter Lakeside Behavioral Hospital. Once I returned back to school, I got into the last physical fight with a classmate, Beth. Many classmates' perception of me, was that I was crazy. There was a lot of name calling with Beth. Some of our mutual friends boosted the fight, but as a result, I won the battle. She left with a busted nose and she left mad because she lost the fight. I later apologized to her at Kroger in Covington during my senior year in college. At that point, Beth and Princess P became friends.

After the mental breakdown my junior year in high school, I went on to successfully graduate in 1997 from Covington High School. From that point, I attended Freshman Studies at the University of Tennessee at Martin and resigned from there in October of 1997. The Lord showed me in another vision that I didn't belong there at UT, so he removed me from the scenery and placed me within Rust College, a historic black college, where I received another taste of being a "child of destiny" and was awarded an UNCF AEGON scholarship for four years.

The question unanswered was, why was my name randomly chosen to receive this scholarship? Attending in 1997, I walked around on campus like I was adored as Queen TLC, I had the Coca-Cola bottle shape, and was fine as wine. Prior to going to Rust, during my last year in high school, I was saved, sanctified, and truly Holy Ghost-filled, but when I transitioned to Rust, the Lord allowed me to fit in by wearing the attire that the students on campus were wearing rather than the skirts I had always worn. Also, he let me truly enjoy the college experience, meeting new friends, socializing, and partying. You can have fun but your inner voice will allow you distinguish right from wrong. He said, "While you were a child, you and your siblings enjoyed the scenery of *A Different World* and were fascinated with the college experience, so I wanted you to relive the dream and not reveal your destiny at the same time."

While on the basketball team at Rust, some teammates used to talk about me during practice, saying that I should attend a twelve-step program because I had dark circles around my eyes. Some stated that I look like I had been using drugs, but I know that wasn't the case. I think some teammates were jealous because they were ugly and needed attention in some way. One of the ladies was tall and looked like a man in drag, so where does she have room to talk about me? Was the word out that I was admired by most on campus? Did she de-grade my name so that she could up-grade hers? This was another case of bullying where a person bullies to shed the light on you and not their own skeletons. By this time, I was a lot stronger against the bullying acts and survived them yet again and moved on to graduate from college in 2001 with my 3.0 grade point average.

CHAPTER 6

GOD'S GIFTED GRADES

Graduating from college with a 3.0 grade point average wasn't the end of my road to the grading system. God said now that you have achieved academic success, I have a grading system that's far better than America's grading scale. My grades differentiate from the school's system. With America, you can pass test with a "C" or higher. Unfortunately, "D" and "F", you have been defeated.

With God's gifted grades, you can pass tests with all grades A through F. Authenticity, bible studying, christianity, discipleship, excellence, and faith. Your daily walk of life must compile of these grades in order to please the master.

Regardless of my struggles with the bullies, I remained true to myself. You have to be real to self first before you can please your higher power. Authenticity is a gift to God. Offering him true genuine love, beautiful has a dove. I want to cling to him like a fish on a hook, through good and bad. A love so deep makes me want to creep, into the daily sea of life during his time. Authorities may charge me with a crime. A crime of passion in many forms of fashion, that filters through my soul and breathes out my nostrils of life.

Bible studying is crucial to daily progress, to a soul that feeds from a foundation of knowledge of his existence during his era. I educate myself daily by reading his word, because I want to die by his sword. I refuse to wait on the Sunday teaching, although heart desires pastoral preaching. Many times we wait on the preacher to provide us the word from God, when we need to learn for ourselves. God did call man to manifest his doctrine and provide biblical refuge. But as judgment day arrives, work as an individual abides in the almighty eyes of the Lord. Your contributions will be questionable. Why didn't you read? As I have given you the loaf of bread, the doctrine of my life.

Christianity plays a key role in discovering the colorful hole in my image, as I become more like Jesus Christ. As I strive for daily perfection, my soul has a powerful connection to a man that's famously known as "The Creator." Now, Satan will try to undermine the "Christ" in "Christian" and make you feel like the last three characters, "ian". I am nothing.

Discipleship with others, form a team that lives a lifestyle free of sin, as the players in the game tries to win. As a disciple of Christ, my primary objective is to win over many souls to Christ and hoping that my life can be magnifying through his light. I want to spread the gospel, share the love and increase connectivity. I lived because he died. My first breath sacrificed his last.

Excellence is a benchmark, set for the high calling and refusing to settle for the falling of the enemy's plan of defeat. I strategize a daily schedule that produces a high quality product and the master has giving a grade "E" for excellence.

Faith of a mustard seed and it grows priceless deed. One that's enrooted in belief that mountains can move, sick can be healed, blind can see, deaf can hear and live a life free of fear. Faith without works is dead. I can't achieve, if I don't believe in a man that created a place we temporarily dwell before walking through heaven stairwell.

Now, I have received my grade from his mid term exam of my life and the grade was, "I" for "Incomplete". God said, "Although you have faith in me", you have failed me miserably by partaking in sexual conduct before marriage. Fornication is a sin and you let the devil deceive you with temptations. I realized that you are sinner before becoming the saint he needs you to be. I lived up to his standards before experiencing seven stages of infatuations and relationships.

I found a small dose of infatuation when I met Mathew. He moved to Covington from Texas and I heard about him from my next door neighbor, Kanisha. One day in science class, she told me that he was so fine that he blew her mind. A couple of days after this information was shared, we ran into each other at Jack's Hall Grocery of Hill and Simelton Streets. He said, "Hey, mama, you look good," and I replied back, "You are, too." He asked for my number. We started talking a little more often and later became a couple. Well, the journey with Mathew would end on a short run. He had started messing with other girls who were close to me, such as my first cousin, Casie. After learning that her mystery name had been revealed, I knew that was my sign that he wasn't for me. God had called on Kanisha to fulfill his journey. Soon after our relationship failed, they found their way into each other's arms. It is so special because that is another example of God's intervention in someone's life. They are still together eighteen years later and happily married with two children. Mathew is now a gospel rap artist.

My second infatuation was Joseph, as I previously discussed (he was the one from the mental breakdown). We were really good friends but he had a girlfriend named Tanisha. He would wait for her to leave the locker and glazed me with his eyes. We would talk on the phone long hours of the night, but he quit associating with me because he thought I was crazy from going to the *nut house*. Joseph is now a movie producer, writer, and artist.

My third encounter was with Ricardo. He had a girlfriend at the time named Diamond. He was later shot and killed from a robbery. I was sad for his loss, but it was his time to go because of the lifestyle he led, hustling in the streets. People always say that if you pass away, that it must have been your time. God shows us that if we live his lifestyle and let him guide our footsteps, we will be at the "right place at the right time." Therefore, he will let you live, walking on the streets covered in glitter and gold. He will never have you in that situation. My revelation from this experience is that Ricardo was at the wrong place at the wrong time.

My fourth infatuation was a small encounter with Otis. This friendship didn't last long because he was not only attracted to me but another church member. I think of him now today as "Supercut." He has a talent of cutting hair and currently has his license to be a barber. We later split paths and I went on to college.

For my fifth infatuation, I left UT Martin and then went to Rust, where I met this guy named Terrance. We met my freshman year. We started connecting in a lot of ways as if it was a mental and emotional rollercoaster. I believe this was the relationship that was allowed before the ultimate challenge of marriage. I had always wanted a set of twins and Terrance gave me that dream. When I found out that I was pregnant, I was excited. The idea of replenishing God's kingdom was amazing. So, I passed the first trimester only to find that when I reached the second trimester, a miscarriage took place. My pregnancy came to a close, but then I found out that I had carried a set of twins. When I was at the hospital, the doctor came in the room and stated, "You have fetus B." I responded, "What do you mean?" She said, "You have twins." I immediately started crying. That was a ride to my journey because of the generational gap from my grandmother, was I meant to only have one child? Also, Terrance had a talent of singing. He sounded like the group Jagged Edge. God showed me a sign when I went to Chicago to visit him and I caught him with another woman in the next room from where I was sleeping. Once I saw that, I ran out, following him, and he turned around and busted me in my eye. His mother gave me an ice pack and sent me back to Memphis on a Greyhound. Also, I never would understand why Terrance would always physically abuse me when other guys would stare at me. We could go anywhere in public or on campus and he would slap me because a guy looked at me and he thought I glazed in another man's eye. He thought I was always disrespecting him, but what was I to do if someone looks at me? Am I not supposed to look at them back? So, he used to have me right these papers on the word *respect.* This relationship molded me for my real man God had for me and how to show respect for my other half.

In my sixth encounter, I met Gottie during my senior year but he had a girlfriend as well. My acquaintance with Gottie was a result of the loneliesness I felt from Terrance. I thought Gottie was sexy and very handsome.

Then, I met Kevin (this was the finale of the infatuation stage). I made it back from Covington the start of my senior year and as I pulled up on campus and put my car in reverse, I ran into his leg. Well, at least I thought I did. He faked the scenery. He played like I ran over his leg to get my attention. Once again, this was another man fascinated by my beauty. So, he got my attention for sure. We started seeing each other at different places. I started tuning in to Kevin's voice because he talked a good game. Little did I know, he was a Q dog (Omega man). So, I believed what he was saying, that he wanted to be with me. Unfortunately, it was later revealed that he had another woman. By that time, I was already infatuated with him.

So somewhere in this mix-up, I should have heard God's voice. I did notice that every time we met up, it was at another one of his frat brothers' houses. I should have listened to the Holy Spirit when he revealed that something was not right about this man. If he says that he wants to be with me, and then why not take me to his home? That's when he told me he was in serious relationship, six months into our friendship. Kevin and I kept in contact up until the final chapter of the destination. I know you are wondering why a "child of destiny" never could get her own man. Well, I later started drifting away from him and his other frat brother was becoming more and more obsessed with me. He would start following me around and it became noticeable with Kevin. They would start to argue over whom I should be with. One was in a very committed relationship and the other was readily available. So one night, I had to meet Kevin over at his frat brother's and he didn't show up. I got angry.

He made excuses why he didn't show and his frat brother tried to take advantage of the no-show and was talking to me, asking me to marry him. This man really was infatuated with me. He asked me to move to Dallas with him, but I said no because I was still hung up on someone else's man. Although I was wrong, it was a journey that came to closure.

You play seconds when you have strong feelings for a man that's really not committed to you. They tell you all the right words, such as "I love you," "I don't want you to be with anyone else," and "I am going to leave my woman one day for you." Also, another familiar set of words will be that they are constantly having problems at home. They tell you all these lies so they can be more active in your life. Little do you know, these men play on your emotions and then when they get caught up and she finds out, you are not going to win. Women with class, decency, dignity, and character about themselves would not play this role because they are considered sloppy seconds to these men. Don't let them tell you that you are going to be his wife one day because he has no intentions of leaving his woman for you. Just wait on the Lord and he will match you with a king that deserves you. For every man there is a woman, and somebody else's man is not the answer you are looking for. I think it is a waste of time messing with these types of men. Stand still and the right man will find you. In the Bible it states, "He that findeth a wife, finds a good thing."

CHAPTER 7

LOVE AT FIRST SIGHT

After all the unsuccessful relationships, I wondered if I would ever find a man of my own. I should be joined with a soul mate to fulfill my destiny. So, confiding in God, I ask him during my senior year if he had plans of marriage in my future. I said, "Let me finish college and then show me a sign at least of a random man." So during my senior year at Rust, I met this guy named Tyrone at Louisiana Pacific in 2001. I was one of three students from Rust that Randstad, a temporary placement agency, had called upon for a three-day job event for this company. Once I started sweeping around the plant, getting it cleaned up, and looking good for the viewers to see the building, I turned around and this man is glazing me through my eyes. He kept following me around and I finally spoke with him. He said, "Hey, lady, how are you doing?" I said, "Fine." Man, I am really glad I stopped by because I had chills run through my body just by looking at him. He was so fine! We took one look at each other and were glazed with one another's presence. So, I had to go finish cleaning up and finish what I started there at LP. During the second day, Tyrone asked me, "Can I kiss you?" I told him no because I don't know you like that, to be interchanging lips and tongues. So, my short bus at that company had come to a red light on the third day. But our love at first sight chemistry and connection that we had was so strong it brought us back together.

The journey to Louisiana Pacific consisted of not only Tyrone and I, but of two other Rust College students named Mike and Sara. The Lord told me through my journey in life that anyone I communicated with would be blessed by the "child of destiny." To this day, they are both happily married to their spouses and living the good life. Mike and Tarsha are both are wonderful teachers and enjoy their jobs. They currently have no children. Also, Sara is my best friend outside of my family members. She has four girls and her husband, Lee is a deacon at their church. He wants a little boy, but is that in God's plan?

So, I hadn't seen Tyrone since my senior year and thought he forgot about my existence. He located me at my first job, at Porter Leath, and took me to lunch. We then started to have more interactions to where I was driving back and forth in 2003 to Holly Springs to visit him at his sister Tamicka's house. I had to keep making the drive until the Lord gave me revelation whether he was going to be my husband. Finally, once it was confirmed, we moved in together. Why not ask the question if it was of God, then why are they shacking? I would say, "You are a sinner before becoming the saint he needs you to be." Excited about the move, we connected on a level that I never felt before. The feeling was like you were on top of the world, above life itself. Once I had encountered this moment, I started to fall more in love with my soul mate. Everything you do together, you will feel the daily connection of being around your soul mate because your souls are intertwined through God's existence. It is so powerful. If you feel really good about this person and you and your soul mate are not married, God's message to you is that you need to wed. In saying that, you can continue to experience this, but it must be only be through holy matrimony from now until death do you part.

After seven stages of infactuation and relationships, I experienced the magical moment only with my soul mate. It wasn't the other seven destiny to satisfy me at such a level only meant for a husband-to-be.

CHAPTER 8

THE MARRIAGE

Tyrone and I later wed in holy matrimony in September of 2003. We fell madly in love with each other way before the wedding, but felt it was best to make it right God's way. This was an episode of Love at First Sight. We loved everything about each other including the flaws and learn to accept the pre-existing conditions. So with that being said, we were faced with the "trial." I had later revealed to Tyrone that I had a gambling addiction. Lord, hear my cry, I don't know how my husband is going to react knowing that I had been taking a lot of my money to Sheraton and Horseshoe Casino. Will my husband continue to stay in our marriage? I called on God many times because it was a habit that I couldn't seem to get rid of. So, once again, the Lord answered my prayer about the marriage. He decided to stay with me and felt that he was going to continue to pray for me daily. With numerous pay periods passing by, I would still be "missing in action." There were times that I felt bad for putting my husband in these situations and decided it would be best for us that I leave for awhile. The Lord showed me one of the many times that I left him that Tyrone would cry. That was my first sign that this was real love in the making. If a spouse expresses love for you through crying or shedding a tear, that is the Holy divine Spirit, always your sign; it's your soul mate. He showed me that this man really loves me. Most men feel that they are too masculine to shed a tear. This was genuine, authentic, soulful love if he shed a tear. It was the first time I ever saw a man cry and Tyrone was my final man after he allowed me to experience the seventh stage of infatuation and relationships. Our love for one another would often remind me of Brooke and Ridge on *The Bold and the Beautiful* daytime drama. These two were destined to be with each other. Love is so real!

Once you find your soul mate and get married, he will allow you to become fruitful through the generational gap. So, four years later after our lifetime commitment to love, honor and cherish life abundantly, we decided that now was a good time to have a child. The marriage was strong and we felt that this was meant-to-be. Our daughter's name is Avriss Jernae Pool. Her first name, Avriss, was selected by Tyrone and her middle name, Jernae, by me. This was a unique name that God spoke through me and allowed her father the opportunity to give her first name and middle name was my calling to make. He gave me the "Jernae" which is another pronunciation of "journey." He said, "Name her this now and I would reveal to you later at the right time the reason why."

Later, in the marriage, Tyrone would start changing, or at least that's what I thought. I would start asking more questions on where he'd been. Why were you gone so long? I noticed increasingly that he would get upset when I just asked a question. It was revealed that Tyrone had a trait that my sister Michelle would possess. The trait commonly known as "I am the nicest person in the world until you press the wrong buttons." One day, he had got so upset from all the questions, he walked out and slammed the door in my face. He didn't come home for the next two days. The arguing made him really upset. It took me by surprise but he said, "I am a man and don't need no questions." After the turning point of the marriage, it came to an intermission stage because I left him again. He would call over and over again but he is the one that walked out and didn't come home for two days. The disagreement really made him upset. So, finally we spoke again and he said, "I need you in my life. You have always been my first love, so I don't want to lose you." He apologized and said, "You have to trust me and not question my whereabouts." I understood his point of view and maybe I was just a little bit insecure considering my previous relationship. So, happily back together, the Holy Spirit revealed that "I can make this work, Tina; you just can't push his buttons like you did Michelle because you see this man more regularly and it could endanger your life if you constantly argue and upset him."

The Trial was the "Marriage and the Ultimate Test" before God put his final print to say, "Love at First Sight" or an "Adam and Eve" example-like couple.

The Tribulation was the "Revelation of God's Intervention" into a marriage that went through many troubles to show that one sign of relief, that this is my calling to be with such a man, have a child through the generational gap, and to live happily ever after. There is no "perfect" marriage; every couple will experience the lows of the "Great Depression Stage," "Natural Disaster," to the "Road to Recovery Stage."

Our "Great Depression" was the gambling addiction and I was spending a lot of my Fridays and Saturdays at the casino. Lady at the Casino would spend a lot of money on the blackjack table. So one day, I was at Sheraton Casino and spent eighteen total hours trying to win back my last couple of dollars. My mother and husband were going to report me missing to the police. So, I finally showed up at home and he was furious, but understanding that I had an addiction. Personally, this was really the only time in my life where I got in a state of depression. I hated living from paycheck to paycheck. It is not a good feeling where you have to get five check advances to make ends meet. My husband would never fight with me, but only worried about where I was. He was always there as a shoulder to cry on.

The "Natural Disaster" was the fact that Avriss inherited epilepsy through the genetic tree of life. I had seizures when I was younger and it was passed on to my daughter. Tyrone would get depressed when she experienced an episode because he thought they were deadly and she was going to die. Although doctors say they are not deadly and she was okay each time, he was worried because that was his baby.

Now, we are on the "Road to Recovery." We can finally breathe again with peace, joy, and fulfillment. "As for me and my house, we will serve the Lord." With him first in your marriage, all these other things will be added unto you!

Through his blessing, we moved out of Memphis, and both got jobs in another state. Where there is a will, there is a way! We moved away from my addiction and life became more fulfilling. There were times that I missed my family and wanted to move back home, but hubby wasn't going for it. As wives, we must satisfy our husbands' needs. If his need is to not go back to Covington or Memphis, you have to follow.

My husband was a professional truck driver and it was kind of hard trusting him over the road. I would go through his phone records and notice numbers he called frequently. It would be women's phone numbers he met over the road. I would call them and get information about the conversation that was exchanged. This is not healthy for any relationship, so I would advise any woman to not invade their spouse's privacy. With a woman's intuition, I came to the conclusion that my husband would only talk to those women because he felt lonely over the road. It is still not right for a spouse to exercise this behavior, but I gave him the benefit of the doubt. I told him it was either me or the women over the road. He chose me. I don't think in our seven years of being married he has physically cheated on me. If you believe in the soul mate destiny, then you would understand why people can be together for years and never cheat on their spouses. The saying "all men cheat" is fictitious.

CHAPTER 9

LOVE TRIUMPHS FAILURE

With the love of the trio—God, Jesus, and the Holy Spirit—I realized my destiny was marked by his territory. During a late intermission stage of my thirtieth year, the Holy Spirit had driven Missionary McCollum to email me on website called Facebook. I hadn't spoke to her in years and all of a sudden out of nowhere, he spoke through her to check on me before the thirty-first year to make sure I was okay because he was going to get me prepared for what was about to happen. But she didn't know that. She was just an angel that he called upon to make an email through a website system. So she emailed and asked, "Tina, are you okay? I was in a prayer meeting at church and the Lord said your name." I said, "Oh, really!" She then said, "Yes, and you are the only Tina I know." My spirit confirmed her honesty.

Also, I remembered a prophet, Evangelist Stokes, in my youth, who said, "She didn't mean you any good." It was later revealed that she meant that because as a "child of destiny," you don't need to hang out with your girlfriends all the time because that demonstrates a dependence on other people to make you complete, whether it be a girlfriend, family member, or a supposed "BFF." You are more an independent character that shouldn't feel the need to be dependent of anyone to make you whole. He said, "Be friends, but I don't need you hanging out each and every day. Because once you find your soul mate in life, they will make you complete in all aspects of life."

God's love for me triumphed over failure because he had two of his angels check on my life during different periods of my thirty year revelation.

Before turning 30, I experienced a dream come true. America elected its first-ever African American King. When God revealed to Obama his calling, the goal was to get prepared as soon as possible. He took the senate seat in Illinois for only two years before getting the big prize God chose for him. He didn't need a tight resume for the position because it was his to begin with. Many pundits thought he would fail because he didn't have enough experience, but God said you have already passed my test. During life, we live day to day making ends meet, trying to connect dot to dot and revisiting the puzzle called "sense of purpose" in life. It takes God to show you the last piece of that puzzle. Once you realize your destiny in life, that must be the ambition every day, seven days a week. If he shows you a vision, it is your responsibility to make it happen as soon as possible. You can't share it with everyone though, because they sincerely won't understand what God has called for you.

I have always been a leader and my message to you is very clear. God's plan for your life is to one day fulfill your mission in life. He has a strategy for all his children, bullied or not. He loves us all, unconditionally. We as of people have been created to minister for a reason, at his given season. Although I made mistakes in my life and committed sins, he remained by my side. God never gave up on me. Each individual have a choice as to which "F" you receive on your report card from the master. "Faith" or "Failure." I chose to have complete faith in our God, that I will see the light at the end of heaven's lane. Failure represents a child that's bullied and commit suicide, lacks high esteem, suffers from depression, or bullys another because they are being bullied. If you chose suicide, you will see darkness through a bottomless pit. Everyone has a voice but make the right choice, the stairwell to heaven.

Researchers for years have been looking for reasons why children are targets of bullying.

Many remain clueless. It has been reported that the five main characteristics of a bullied child is: Sensitivity, socially withdrawn, they tend to think poorly of themselves, quiet temperament, and more likely to be depressed. Well, this wasn't my case at all. I was very intelligent, sociable, people's person, thought very highly of myself, talkative, humorous, and never depressed. Also, recognized by some peers that my personality remained the same regardless of the situation. I didn't appear to be fake, to become noticeable. You either loved me or hated me because I wasn't going to try and please man.

The latest statistics show that 85 percent of children are bullied today and 32 percent of parents fear their child safety at school. A child commits suicide as a direct result of being bullied once every half hour. My heart aches thinking of those statistics. For a child to bully another child to a level of suicide, that is a "devil's advocate." Just as the Devil is looking for employees daily, God is searching for leaders, top executives to save his children from the pain and suffering. I have been hired by God to fulfill a destiny. Our kids will start looking in the mirror daily, seeing "revisions" and feeling, "revived." You will hear the same tune but with a different face.

A lot of famous people today have overcome bullying and have achieved success. Whitney Houston, Michelle Pfeiffer, Michael Phelps, Kevin Costner, Christian Bale, Clay Aiken, Christina Aguilera, Chris Rock, Tiger Woods, President Bill Clinton and President Barack Obama. We are all able to say, "we are survivors of this race." Will you join our "amazing grace?"

CHAPTER 10

FIGHT AGAINST BULLYING

On the day of my thirty-first birthday, the Spirit wanted me to wake up, get beautified, and take pictures before sunup and when I went out and celebrated my birthday (as a representation of sundown). In these photos, I would exemplify the beauty that would be needed to receive the rest of the plan. "I wanted to show you the meaning behind the 'unpretty' to the 'pretty' transformation. I can change you within one day, but to many it would feel like a thousand years.

So, now, the day after your thirty-first birthday, I showed you a vision of a book and a successful business plan. You have always worked the jobs I selected you to employ and they were:

1.) Porter Leath Children Center, a child-based company
2.) Adesa Memphis, car industry, global company
3.) ServiceMaster, global company
4.) HCA Physician Services, global healthcare
5.) Holladay Properties, healthcare properties

Through those five companies, I had you experience the strongest and weakest in terms of customers/client base. So your empire that will be built will surpass that journey of employment that I put together in the past. The economy is the main focus today and we need a *niche* created to help achieve that goal. Now, I've allowed you to get your degree in accounting plus nine years under your belt so you can have the resume set for the job I need you and your families to perform."

My empire will be built around who I am, what I stand for, and Whom I live for. It will be called "The TLC Organization." It will be focusing first on the needs of children and fighting against bullying, cyberbulling, and violence in schools and on helping to decrease the high statistics. Polls show an alarming 85 percent of students in school today are bullied. Nearly 25 percent have attempted suicide but have failed.

This all would be revealed in his plans, and then when I knew it was the Holy Spirit driving my force within nature, the "Hidden Secret" was revealed. "Your spirit will confirm and cite different examples of visions he showed you during your thirty-year prep period.

Now, this business plan that he showed me through a vision on August 15, 2010, would be fourteen different business lines, such as family reunions, weddings/receptions, rip the catwalk, talent shows, high school events, baby/bridal showers, kid events, weekly parties for partygoers, church picnics, birthdays/anniversaries, and comedy events, but is that really in the plan? All of these business lines demonstrate the key importance of family unity, intervention, providing extracurricular activities for kids and teens, showing their elegance in stage modeling, celebrating newborn babies, weddings of whom God put together, and discovering hidden talents in our youth. But are these some lines of business that will create jobs within today's weakened economy?

This plan illustrates different niches that will create jobs and in order for a business to grow and succeed, one must have multiple revenue lines. The first company I worked for is a child-based company that services the needs of children from Bright Start to foster care programs. The second company services top dealerships such as Chrysler, Toyota, GM, Nissan, etc., in the auto/auction industry. The third company is one of the strongest in terms of revenue, and services the industries of termite control, landscaping,

Merry Maids, and so on. This company has ten different service units. The fourth company administers to health needs of Americans all across the world. Last but not least, the fifth company services the property management industry and is the weakest in terms of all the jobs I've been employed for. My employment history consists of some of the best companies in terms of a strong base and one that exemplifies a weak base (because it has one main client that could pull out from business any day).

The TLC Organization has future plans of becoming global, but I have to start small. We will assist parents and children. TLC will teach many things, but first the success of self-awareness. If you love yourself, cherish everything about yourself, and know yourself, whether good or bad, then you can build high self-esteem off those three ingredients. Once you have accomplished the fundamentals, then when someone bullies you, those evil words will be meaningless. My mentorship program will guide you in all the right directions.

I knew myself and capitalized on those key moments. Every time my bullies harassed me, mentally I spoke, "That's not me." They told me over, over, and over again, "You are so ugly. You are not pretty enough." Or, "You look like someone has taken their car and ran over you. You look like a raccoon with those two black eyes." Those are the lyrics that I literally heard every week at school. Still with God's love that triumphs failure, I was able to overcome the embarrassment, humiliation, and drama all those years from fifth grade to my sophomore year in college. It will be an honor to assist families through these times.

Tina was my bullied-stage name and Queen TLC was my name that was earned during the survival stage. I defeated my bullies. Never in a million years would I have figured out my plan for my life without God's helping hand. I said life isn't supposed to be like this. When I looked in the mirror, I saw a woman of beauty, elegance, dignity, and who was highly favored. You feel superior in God eyes, but the devil (bullies) wants you to feel inferior.

In life, you may never pay attention to the signs (astrology) until he shows you the other side of your character. I am a Leo (birth date August 14) and was born to lead. It was in my genes. The bullies saw what God instilled in me and wanted to de-grade me by all means. I received my report card from the Man upstairs and it had "Grade A" written all over it. It represented my path to success, authenticity, accountant, and author.

In my eyes, a bully is 3D: dysfunctional, distant, and disconnected. Those traits are commonly possessed by the devil. Just as God has his children, the devil has many as well. These bullies are young and don't understand that these are demons that have taken over their minds. Your enemies don't want you to succeed and they thrive off your failures. If a bully can take any ounce of your dignity, he or she has won you over and will move onto the next victim.

Dysfunctional is rooted in the home environment. If a person does not get the feeling of belonging and love at home, this child will act out to find his place in society. It starts with the parents and filters its way through the school system.

Distant means distance from God because he said, "Love thy neighbor." Thy neighbor doesn't necessarily just mean your next door neighbor, it could be a student that you sit beside in class every day, or a student that your locker is next to, or a person whom you randomly walk by day to day. How could you say "I love God" if you boldly take advantage of a student every day and you have never seen God?

Disconnected means that you are detached from people and you lack the love of people. If you have love in your heart, you would treat others the way you feel. It is hatred for humans when you do everything in your power to de-grade their character. You try to make them feel helpless, defeated, and disgusted.

During my time, it appeared that Tina was the only target. I never saw anyone else getting bullied like me. They were waiting on me at all cost. If it meant being late for their classes, it didn't matter to them as long as I was heartbroken.

Mark and Brian shared five common traits: lack of strong family unity, lack of physical happiness, lack of social happiness, lack of high self-esteem, and lack of peer acceptance. In order for them to get the proper respect from peers, they made others laugh and brought humor at the lockers, games, and classroom by putting down an innocent student. Otherwise, people would have not been drawn to them like a magnet because they were social misfits and lacked external attractiveness. Their friends finally accepted them, played their games, and crowned them with the devil's horns.

I have never felt a need to talk about anyone because I felt I had it all together and didn't need to put someone else down to make myself feel better. When I studied the main ones that bullied me, Mark actually looked like a bull. With his numerous amounts of teeth, he would bite you at any given time.

"Let's go to school and play with her emotions." A lot of my so-called friends were laughing right with them in my face. I had gotten into so many fights that they called me "Miss Mike Tyson." The fights are over, but the scars remain for life. This was a representation of the battles one faces when one is constantly being bullied.

The teachers didn't do anything. Back in the day, many felt that it wasn't serious enough to take the time out to counsel. Their approach was, "That's what youngsters do. Some will fight and make up the next day." Well, that wasn't the case. We didn't make up the next day and what if I didn't believe in God or have high self-esteem? This could have been a tragic suicide case and breaking news on CNN.

During grammar school, I was always in honor classes. I was excelling right with the white students, and oftentimes I would let them cheat off my papers. With my mindset, I always felt a need to help others. So, you see, I always felt superior to others because of the drive, the need to be the best I can be. Some of my white friends would say, "You are a sweetheart." I always had this crush on this white boy and we were both smart, but I believe he was ashamed of me.

It is time to take action against the bullies. The TLC Organization will take pride in helping schools fight against bullying. We must believe that bullying deteriorates the human brain and act accordingly. Students should report all cases, whether as an innocent bystander or the victim of bullying. The bully should receive detention and be dealt with by the state laws. Currently there are only a few states that have adopted laws, but others need to take on the issue more aggressively. Stop thinking that these are minor cases and do something because what if it was your child that came home from school to hang herself? Or she could have come home from the library, went in your room, found your pistol and said, "Dad, look at me," and blew her brains out right in front of you. How would you feel then? Are we being selfish because they are not our children? Shouldn't school officials be held accountable for their misinterpretation of this worldwide crime?

Should schools start teaching an optional class on religion and self-awareness?

Teach our kids the true meaning of having a higher power in their life and the importance of building their foundation on a rock that no person can tear down at their leisure, especially if it is not being taught at home.

Students are afraid to go to school and not focus on their studies 100 percent. How can they be inspired to take their education to the next level? I believe students are very intelligent but are distracted that the next guy is writing notes to other students about the victim and everyone's giggling about the name-calling. Our schools should be the base of tomorrow's leaders—the next engineer, accountant, teacher, politician, writer, or chief executive.

We will be a force to be reckoned with, working with school officials to decrease the dramatic rates of bullying and dropping out. Bullying is a factor of students dropping out of school. All it takes is for everyone to be on board from parents, superintendents, and teachers. Enough is enough! We can't stop the devil in his ways of bullying, but we can teach the child what to do if they are being bullied. Never give up on your life!

CHAPTER 11

THE REVELATION

Once the revelation had been revealed that I was a "child of destiny," I knew I was in for a longer journey. He had placed a call of anointing on my life that was better than life itself. In the King James Version of the Revelation, he said that some will be walking on the streets of gold. This will be a new, profound era on heaven and earth in 2010.

Both of my grandmothers were a true inspiration in my life. My mother's mother died during the Bush era in 1991, and my dad's mom passed during the first year of the Obama era in September 2008 (one year after my daughter, Avriss, was born). She was blessed to live here over three scores and ten and more. When she was laid to rest, it was a day I will never forget. Through the generational gap, she passed her torch onto me to do a better job than she did.

The Holy Spirit finally showed me what my true calling/meaning in life was. It was to become a successful writer and be an advocate for bullying. I will write as the Holy Ghost gives me guidance. Also, I will be a witness/service his people through the meaning of his Word and my testimony. He waited until the time was right. Every time I turn on the television, I see numerous cases of children being bullied and committing suicide. My voice shall be heard because I have experienced the same pain they are going through and came out a survivor.

See, you have to know that he is a God of patience. You must wait until you are called upon or chosen to perform a position within his administration. "Many are called but few are chosen." The Lord called upon Hillary Clinton to run for the democratic presidential nomination, but it wasn't her time to win. Although she was a good candidate for the job and gave Obama the best competition for the race, that wasn't her position to win. So, he gave her a position within Obama's team (as Secretary of State), but not the Head of State. Many people, to this day, don't understand why two people can go head to head in competition for a primary and still be friends like Obama and Clinton. It was Hillary's calling for Secretary of State at this crucial time in America. Obama needed someone with a strong foreign policy background. Hillary was the best fit in God's eye. The presidency should only be held by a man. So, during the Bush era, God was prepping Obama for his true calling in life. Many may think Obama will only be a one-term president; I predict today that he will be a two-term president through God's love, it will triumph failure. He has chosen him to complete his eight-year destiny as a US president.

The King James Version of the Bible stated how people would speak in unknown tongues that the Spirit gives them the utterance for. This book is a testimony to that fact because a successful writer will be Holy Ghost-driven to write the foundation of a book in three days. My senior year in college and writing my accounting internship paper was the last time I wrote for days and nights. This is because my family thought I was crazy when discussing the details; my tongue was speaking in an unfamiliar tone and they never heard me talk this way. Richard said, "You are crazy; your tone of voice is different and we need to take you back to the *nut house.*" Some people don't understand that when God shows you the calling on your life, you should run with it and don't waste time.

Let your light shine through others because you can be a witness to his Word and have your own testimony to tell. People feed off testimonies because that is a test of life. During my journey, it was discovered that he chose me to be a witness that he is real. Many people don't believe in him until someone shares her destiny.

During my 1990s era, I remembered that there was a renewed sense of peace, unity, and happiness on earth. It felt the same way the week of my vision, from August 15 through 21, 2010, as if the world was headed in that direction. Some of the most popular singing groups from those times are now going to revive their talents and entertain the world all over again. Your breaking period has ended. We will relive the sense of belief in our economy again as we did in the 1990s. Americans will be proud to get up and go to work. The unemployment rate will begin to decrease because employers will be entrusted to start back hiring again. All of this would be revealed to me during day one through day seven of his plans. I had to remind myself that it was 2010 and not the 1990s because it felt so real. He was prophesying the tasks ahead for the next couple of years.

Being successful means you are given your own success story. Not because you clock in and out every day, but each in generation, a successor(s) is named with a different story to tell. A successor can be someone that writes your story, sings about your life, etc. Everybody can't have the same story to tell, that is why we live in "A Different World."

One of the famous people I am truly inspired by is Mary J. Blige. Her career in singing started during the 90s when I had the first vision of fame. She sang as the Spirit gave her utterance to song write and sing not only about her life, but other human beings experiencing the same obstacles she faced. Her music guided and directed me during that phase of my life. She was one of those whom wrote my life through song and ministry. The albums *What's the 411* and *Stronger with Each Tear* testify this fact. During each phase of my life, a song was played that helped me get through a struggle or a love triangle. When you are a bullied child, some of your favorite music will help keep your mind off what the bullies are saying. You will play the track over and over again. Princess P use to always say, "Girl, didn't you just hear that song?" I would respond by saying,

"It helps detour my mind from negative and think about positive, soulful music that I can relate to."

Most famous people are considered to be "destiny children" because in his Word (Matthew 6:33), God talks about how if you seek him first then all these other things shall be added unto you. Your life is already planned for you (Matthew 25: 14–30); those who are talented and gifted will be blessed accordingly. If you allow the Holy Ghost to lead and guide you, then those with two talents will be blessed with two more, those with five will be given five more, but the one wicked and lazy servant with one talent, that talent will be taken away. This parable relates to denomination of money but if you are talented and famous, monetary value is produced from the gift. All of the individuals have touched someone's life and made it a better heaven and earth as God did. "Everything you touch or encounter will be blessed."

He has revealed that I have the talent of braiding hair professionally, accountancy, and now the gift of writing. God is an on-time god. He will not necessarily come when you want him, but he is always on time. That saying means that when you pray for him to come your way, he might not show up at that given time, but right when you need him is when he answers your prayers. He comes through the most needed moment. During the week after my thirty-first birthday, he showed me the talent of writing and told me that he wasn't done with me yet. I have more undiscovered talent yet to be revealed. All my life, I have walked the walk and talked the talk. See, he knows your heart and if you are real with him during life, he will bless you with the Holy Spirit. Once you receive this gift, it will put everything in perspective in terms of history, the current century we live in, people, why we live the way we live, the challenges, and all of humanity.

People I have known always say that famous people are going to die and go to hell because they have profited the whole world and lost their souls. This saying is true in some sense, depending on the individual. They are just living the life on the big screen because they were blessed with God's talent to be a guide and role model to others. Most have talents to sing, dance, act, produce, mentor, edit, and write. When God's behind your talents, you will be blessed with multiple. Now, if your work is driven for monetary value, then that saying is true. Your initiative must be in the essence of his existence and changing the lives of others every day like he did.

CHAPTER 12
THE VISION

In the Bible, God stated he created heaven and earth in six days and named the final day the Sabbath. He has given the "child of destiny" an "ultimate test."

This was to fulfill the need of creating my own "Old" and "New" Testaments of my thirty-year lifetime of events. His plan had been revealed and outlined as follows:

Day 1-First day after your thirty-first birthday, your third talent of writing has been revealed. Previous two talents, gift of professionally braiding hair and gift of accountancy.

Day 2-More revelation has been revealed about my plan for you. Also, reveal the real reason why bullied children are targets of such negative behavior.

Day 3- Complete the foundation of your new book, *Diary of a Bullied Child: The Aftermath.*

Day 4- Increased your maturity level of a plan to achieve the impossible.

Day 5-"The "Resignation." Your last employer was Holladay Properties and, in order for you to leave in a "High Call" manner, present them with the "presentation" of publishing your new book. Staff will think you are crazy for doing so, but you are not here to please man. Follow my lead. They will reject the idea because they don't have the capabilities of publishing a book. This will allow you to resign where the company has no record of you quitting or getting fired. You have accomplished the challenge of being a portfolio accountant. I have chosen you to perform a "global portfolio." Bullying is a global issue and we need advocates that are survivors.

Day 6-Finalize the foundation of your new book and make the appropriate changes.

Day 7-Please rest/ breaking point for the task ahead.

CHAPTER 13

THE RED CARPET

Fame starts with a vision from God, and I was getting prepared for what was about to happen in my life and the effect of my family's journeys. The platform had already been set when he showed me Tina Turner and TLC during my childhood through visions back in my 1990s era. One of my key values has always been "love thyself before you can love another human being" and the spirit translation of "unpretty" to "pretty."

God is so real because now I understand the meaning behind my fascination of becoming a member of Delta Sigma Theta sorority. I applied for this organization during my sophomore year and got rejected. The color of DST is red, and although I failed the first try, he set it up for me to try again. The next time he said, "You will be a Star on my Red Carpet." It's like the red carpet is being rolled out in front of my "black eyes" as he continues to reveal my destiny. He didn't want the "child of destiny" a part of that organization; it wasn't his will.

In college, people were becoming members of organizations to make them feel superior and a part of a sisterhood. I didn't need the three letters, DST, to make me feel higher than peers. Usually, those organizations are self-esteem boosters for most and competition to others, but just think about it. About 80 percent of the members of Delta Sigma Theta from Rust, when they became alumni, were not active in their communities and didn't pay their fees. Now, if they were true to their organization, regardless of graduate fees, they should pay whether they can afford it or not.

As a "child of destiny," I felt superior to all because he has given me a feeling that surpasses DST, Zeta, Alpha Kappa Alpha, and so on. He has molded me into a beautiful woman that has self-love, high self-esteem, and high honor.

Delta Sigma Theta did me a favor by rejecting me because I didn't need an esteem booster. Most women on Rust campus enjoyed wearing the three letters because they needed something to lean on when they couldn't count on themselves to succeed. They looked for an outlet to receive attention; otherwise they wouldn't get any at all.

The organization itself stands for more than esteem booster, but economic and educational development, international awareness, physical and mental health, and political awareness and involvement. If you are joining to make a difference in the community, I highly respect those individuals. Otherwise, if you join for the wrong reasons such as boosting oneself, you should count on the Man above to serve his purpose.

It was the red blood of Jesus on the rejection letter from DST. He had another plan for my life and didn't need DST on my resume to get the job that was meant for me. My destiny had already been planned. Although, personally, DST was my answer to service the needs of children and help in the community, he chose another route, which was the Upward Bound program where I assisted disadvantaged youth at Rust. I enjoyed mentoring to the children and developing ways to enhance reading and mathematical skills. My favorite mottos in life: "Live each day to the fullest, as if it was your last" and "What can I do to touch the lives of other human beings?"

CHAPTER 14

SOLVED MYSTERY

Looking at the Man up above, I told him, "The queen has solved the mystery." After graduating from college, I started my first job in accounting on May 7, 2001, at Porter Leath Children's Center and the last stop was at Holladay Properties on April 7, 2008.

I got the first job a week after graduating from college and the last job the same day I interviewed for the job. During my first book, he revealed the symbolic meaning behind the numbers because the first and the last start day was on the number seven. It was marked by his blood.

I spoke to the Lord numerous times during the last destination stop, which was Holladay Properties, that something had to change. I would clock in and knew that I should be clocking in on someone else's clock, but didn't know what employer was waiting on my ambitious mind of talent. From the point of being hired, everything would be okay until I was a little bossy and felt my supervisor lacked skills in the accounting area. The Holy Spirit showed me that Holladay was only a "temporary job until you are ready for the permanent one." I was written up once because I would talk about my supervisor. I felt she did a horrible job and often spoke sarcastically about her work ethics. I said that if I had to give her a grade that it would be a C- and that would be for just showing up. We didn't get along because I felt she disrespected me by partaking in unethical behavior. Also, there were times I was being picked on from managers misinterpreting emails and any form of my communication. Every employer that has ever evaluated me stated that I was like a "perfect employee" that got the job done right. Most would see me as striving to be a perfectionist. But the last three jobs all had something in common. They found a negative critique and said that "your communication can be improved upon." Which is totally understandable, but God was showing me that in order to be a writer, one must supersede the oral and written communication expectations.

Each job that was a part of my journey also symbolized a sibling in some way. Porter Leath Children's Center—Joe was the miracle baby; ADESA Memphis car/ van industry—Princess P was a US Postal Service worker; Service Master—Richard was servicing the needs of the "child of destiny" all his way, whether it was from grammar school to college years; HCA Physician Services—Kelly currently holds a position as a nurse; and Holladay Properties—John never established a solid work history. He was enjoying a holiday— unpaid leave most of his days.

That's when the Lord revealed my other talent as a writer because he knew my gifts were far superior to my job description as an accountant. This was the Lord's way of letting me know that I was about to have a "Holladay" on God's "Property."

With his continued revelation, it was impossible for me to get any sleep. I was faced with insomnia because I lacked sleep for seven whole days. Doctors prescribed a sleeping pill that cost $600. I had resigned from my employer and later had to go back because not only was it a good company, but the insurance I had for almost three years would take care of my expensive medicine.

Now, this is the same problem Michael Jackson (RIP) faced. He continued to ask for sleep medicine from his doctor and later overdosed. His doctor was only doing what he was asked and he didn't kill Michael. With his tour schedule and his need to practice before performance time, he was faced with the impossible. Insomnia will make you feel helpless and there is no way you can perform at that level with no sleep. His case should be closed forever and let his name rest in peace.

As I look back over my life and the many encounters, I notice that everyone I came in contact with was blessed and talented. Out of them all, I am glad to know that the guy that took my virginity is still with Kanisha (who was my next door neighbor). They have been together ever since I broke up with him. Most people think I betrayed Kanisha, but it was a part of my journey.

The guy named Mark (who graduated with me) that made the ugly song "TINA the Termite" about me is still single and miserable. He tries to find all these activities, such as basketball and being an Omega man, to fill a void in his life. So, really you can't be evil to God's chosen ones and be blessed in life. I never cried about being bullied, which showed how strong I was. I could have talked about the fifty-two teeth he had on his front plate, but I chose not to be evil like him. We are Facebook friends now, but I will never forget the song during childhood! He bullied me to put peers' attention away from his own skeletons, such as the way he looks, his character, and the demons he possesses. I have learned that if you have several imperfections, one must shift directions so that their obviousness doesn't become the topic of discussions.

I later discovered that I had bipolar disorder/mania. Now, for most, it would be categorized as a mental illness, but some people with the disease will find out that it is a "disease for the geniuses." These human beings have supernatural qualities and would be the masterminds/owners behind the companies you work for, the global businesses within our economy, who created the vehicles you drive. Also, many famous people are believed to have been affected by this disorder. It is often suggested that this is associated with creative talent, specifically the mania side of bipolar disorder.

I am a "child of destiny" and for the most part, have a high self-esteem that no man can tear apart! I adore myself, and when I look at what God has done, it was a miracle! When I checked into the hospital to get caught up on my sleep, all the other patients were there because they had low self-esteem, depression, and suicidal thoughts and needed some direction in life. All the workers at the hospital knew I was a different breed and they used me as an example to the other patients to help teach their twelve-step program. Once again, family members thought I was crazy but never understood the calling that I had on my life! During day two through day six, it rained in Nashville continuously. One of the parents at the daycare stated, "I wish the rain would go away." After she made the comment, God revealed later that day the reason for the rain. Once his child has been told through the Holy Ghost his calling for your life, it will rain until he has you on board with his plan. Now, most people wouldn't understand this unless you have been shown through vision and believe in God. It didn't rain on the first day or the last day. It is now time to let my light shine and get to God's business. It is my destiny to serve him, so let's have a Holy Ghost party!

Are you still clueless about your life's purpose? Well, we all have the same thoughts about life in general. Humans ponder over and over again about how our lives should be. Isn't there more to life than going to work every day, looking at TV, spending time with family, or just simply hanging out with friends?

Well, the answer is now available through the *Diary of a Bullied Child*. It is worth living a dramatic, action-filled, and suspenseful life until your true destiny is revealed. Why do you say that? Life is a movie. You have a main character/star, supporting actor or actress, characters that are killed off, and survivors of the storyline.

My movie demonstrated that through the generational era, each star had their moment. My grandmother was the star/main character in her era and lived for seventy-nine years and everything that she touched turned to gold. Also, she was the angel of fourteen kids. All her family and friends were "touched by an almighty angel." She had a supporting cast during her time and some cast members died off the set, such as her brothers, sisters, and friends. Now, the main star of the family will only be allowed to have one to three kids at the most. It is the job of the supporting cast to be fruitful and replenish the family legacy.

Through the generational gap, God allowed my grandmother to pass her blood to me, that I would be enriched by her existence. The main character of the movie never dies off until they have lived at least their three scores and ten. They will live to see their great grandchildren.

I was the star of my parents' seven kids. My supporting cast was everyone that I interacted with, whether it was family, friends, enemies, or lovers. See, my grandmother didn't have any enemies, but I did. It was a part of my storyline that my enemies were my bullies. He allowed me to experience every part of my life from the bullying, fornication, suffering, pain, and the dramatics so that my storyline will be more powerful than ever.

God revealed that majority of *truly* bullied children are chosen to be superstars. Many are called, but only few are chosen. These children are very different, unique, mentally fit to lead, don't need peer acceptance, don't try to please man, and wait till it's their time to be in the spotlight. They are typically the ones, that don't fit in with their peers, which make them more noticeable as targets. Usually in the average environment, observe the bullies that are trying to fit in at all costs, getting in the "popular" spotlight. It means putting down another peer or bystander laughing to get noticed. The bullied child has ambition, charisma, drive for success that goes very deep on the inside, it shines so bright, and overshadows the bullies light. They will endure what I have discovered through my experience, "bull fever."

When you know God, he will allow you to connect the dots and then it will symbolize the globe and become a "global message."

No one will ever compare to God (the father) and Jesus (the Son), but those he has chosen will reach, change, and empower the minds of this world we call heaven and earth with their message.

When I think back to when I was a bullied child, during those tough times, I never knew why movies and music would comfort me so abundantly. People like Mary J. Blige, Whitney Houston, R. Kelly, Michael Jordan, Sylvester Stallone, and Arnold Schwarzenegger all had something common.

My favorite movies of all time were, "The Bodyguard," "Commando," and "Rocky IV."

Those movies symbolized to me that "God is your bodyguard; he commands you to follow his footsteps, and it is going to literally feel like a boxing match in a ring." When one experiences bullying, that is exactly what it feels like and it is very painful. You are constantly getting a punch to the head.

My favorite singers of all time, and people that I know would say that it is true, are Mary J. Blige and R. Kelly. I never knew why I was so fascinated with their success until days after my thirty-first birthday. R. Kelly is the best male R & B singer of his time and Mary J. Blige is the best female R & B singer of her time. These are icons and their legacies will be cherished forever. When I reviewed each album title for Mary, her songs symbolized a special moment in my life.

Michael Jordan and the Chicago Bulls were my favorite basketball team of all time. I used to cry every time Michael lost a single game. He meant so much to me. When he left the Bulls, so did my love for the game of professional basketball. Now when I think about the animal bull, my first campaign will be, "No More Bull-ying" in our schools! This animal poses a threat to society and so does human bullying. Our children are our future and to make them stronger in academics, we must tackle the issue of bullying. Teachers, teacher aides, principals, and superintendents of schools must address these issues immediately. Our children shouldn't be afraid to go to a certain class or fear going to public libraries or their lockers or an after school event because they are terrified of facing a dysfunctional, distant, and disconnected bully. Once this problem is dealt with wholeheartedly, America will notice that more kids will graduate, less will drop out, and kids will not be hesitant about going to school daily.

So what does all this mean? The difference between actual movies and our lives is that they're acting knowingly and in real life we don't know that we are acting out our lives. Your life is somebody's movie, whether it is on the big screen or the small television.

When God reveals your lifetime of events, you will sigh a sigh of relief to yourself: "Oh that makes perfect sense!" Unfortunately, the events will be horrifying, action-filled, dramatic, suspenseful, or comical.

In my movie, Ricardo, a supporting actor, got killed off the scene due to him being at the wrong place at the wrong time. Princess P, supporting actress, got shot and killed as well. She was at the right place at the wrong time. I say that because she loved her job at the US Postal Service. She went in early one day and the shooters came to kill her and another innocent coworker in Hennings, Tennessee. Princess P was my best friend and I loved her to death. They are both gone but never forgotten. Ricardo and Princess P's deaths had the same cause of death. The killers motive was robbery.

With God in your heart, he will lead you through the path of righteousness. If you live by his commandments and listen to his voice, your destiny will be fulfilled. You will feel like you are walking into a new heaven and earth. You will see life in a better light and he will continue to guide you. When he gives you the power of the Holy Ghost, you will always be at the right place at the right time.

SETTING THE STAGE

Part II of a bullied child will address bullying in more depth. This book will change and educate the minds of parents and school officials. It is very important to study bullying in the day-to-day operations of your home and school.

Right now, the world views bullying as a situation in which the bullied child is chosen by a bully because of distinctive outer appearances or stereotypes, such as being ugly; having an unattractive hairstyle; being fat; being skinny; being gay; having big ears, a big nose, or big lips; being disabled; having different clothes; etc.

Well, my experience in this subject matter tells me that bullies choose their victims very wisely. Not all children are bullied. Some are teased from time to time, but others are targets all the time. Bullies tease different students before they detect the actual target. Once they have selected the target, that's their passion throughout the school year. Why was the target chosen? Is there something wrong or dysfunctional about the bullied child? Is there a particular reason they are picked on constantly?

All of the articles, books, and pundits speculate the reasons and take different polls to test the deep issue of why, out of one-hundred students, two or three are chosen as targets. They say bullied children are more likely to be socially withdrawn, sensitive, and depressed and have low self-esteem. More than likely, if a child is harassed constantly and doesn't have a solid foundation for himself or herself, then this poll seems somewhat accurate.

As discussed in Part I, there are internal qualities that a bullied child possesses that shine so brightly that the lights will suddenly appear to be on everywhere they go. Young children have an inability to identify these internal instincts but do feel like outcasts among peers. I felt this way every day at school. My ambition, willpower, and charisma were instilled inside, and there's nothing anyone can do to change that. We were "born to shine." At the end of each day, you feel like a "shining star" regardless of what the bullies may think. When your foundation is built on rock, sticks and stones will never break your bones.

If my parents had been aware of the bullying and wanted me to change schools to escape the horror, I still would have been a target at other schools because of who I was born to be. After reading Part II, Smell of Stardom, you will definitely know why bullies choose their victims wisely.

PART 2

SMELL OF STARDOM

CHAPTER 15
THE SYMBOLISM

The day before I had the vision of fame at sixteen, I went to the Player's Club in Jackson, Tennessee, with my cousins Monifah and Martha. We had a ball dancing with the guys, laughing and enjoying the moment. We had several drinks but remained very attentive to our environment. As the disc jockey played the last song, "Slow Dance," by R Kelly, I took the dance floor with this guy named Joe. He whispered sweet things in my ear, but I didn't give into the temptations of the Player's Club. This is where the players prey on vulnerable young girls. Monifah and Martha were ready to go, tired from all the dancing, but they waited at the door for me to finish my last dance. As the song finished, Joe told me, "I saved the last dance just for you." I responded by saying, "Our paths will cross again if it's meant to be." As we exited the building, I realized I left my drink on the table. I didn't go back and get it because someone could have put a drug in my cup. Oh, that could really harm me. I was having so much fun and was so entertained by the pleasures of the Player's Club that I left a drink unattended that I had just paid for. Well, Martha, Monifah, and I returned to their parents' house to go to sleep. Monifah said, "Goodnight, because I am wore out from the dance floor." The next morning, it was time for me to go back home to Covington.

The day after I left Jackson with my cousins, my family said I had started having visions of fame. I thought my sisters and I were the group TLC. I felt famous, and walking the streets of Covington, I was faced with people laughing at me and thinking I was crazy. The magic that I was feeling was if I were imaging the future, my destiny of a higher calling.

Several days passed, and I was still on a heavenly high and believing I was getting married to my high school sweetheart, Joseph. After getting into a fight with Beth, my parents drove me to Charter Lakeside Hospital for a little while. Family members had spread rumors that someone at the club put something in my drink. How could that be so if I didn't go back and get the drink that was left unattended? Doctors diagnosed that I had a chemical imbalance. Did God have a different diagnosis?

Fifteen years later, I had the same experience. During the seven days in 2010 from August 15–21, God revealed my destiny in life: becoming a successful writer and servicing the needs of bullied children. We must teach them that their destiny can't be fulfilled if they commit suicide at the hands of bullies.

The week my destiny was revealed, I felt like I was in heaven, as God prophesized the real meaning of life, why we exist, the history of generations, and the curse of destiny. He revealed revelation that most people wouldn't understand in a natural sense but that one can only comprehend with supernatural powers. You have to be deeply enrooted in God and have the Holy Ghost to understand the symbolism of life. Everywhere you go, people you connect with randomly, and your place in family history all symbolize something in life. The average person will concur that life's events happen coincidentally, for no apparent reason beyond nature.

My bullying experience happened for a reason. It happened so that I could be an inspiration twenty years later, at a time where God's children are affected by this crime more than ever. God instilled stardom, charisma, and ambition in my mind, body, and soul. My bullies detected my internal traits and wanted to make me feel inferior because I was "born superior."

As a child, you can't correlate the reasons until your higher power connects the dots for you. He allows you to connect the dots of life when the time is appropriate. It must be in his time. The Chicago Bulls symbolized the "bull" in *bully*. *Rocky IV* symbolized the experience of bullying in a boxing match: bullies continue to deliver a blow to the head with their evil words and physical fights, and it ruins you mentally for life. If you don't have a permanent bandage for the damage, the brain damage never heals.

If he guides your footsteps, you are always at the right place and right time. The night of my thirty-first birthday, I went to the Player's Club in Nashville, Tennessee, with Matty and Marcia. These are the other two sisters of Monifah and Martha. God revealed my destiny/calling in life the next day. He puts you in different scenes in life for a reason. He knows exactly what he's doing.

These two defining moments in my life have something in common. When I was sixteen, he revealed the vision of fame. At turning thirty-one, he revealed my destiny. The day before both events, I went to the Player's Club with a different set of sisters from the Richmond family. Why was that so, when these are the only two times in our lives that I ever hung out with my cousins in Jackson and Nashville?

During my thirty-year lifetime, I was hospitalized the week after each defining moment. Taking me in 1995 to Charter Lakeside Hospital and in 2010 to Vanderbilt Psychiatric Hospital, my family drove me to a place where God revealed what heaven really is. It is so magnificent spiritually because it felt like an unbelievable dream. During the last hospital visit in 2010, he showed me that my dead grandmother would be the one to open the gates of heaven for me when I leave this world. I knew it was her because I recognized the voice, but I only saw her young face, the face I'd seen in one of her high school photos. My grandmother died when she was seventy-nine years old, but when she welcomes me into heaven, she'll have a face that is so young. I said, "Granny, that's you." She replied by saying, "Come here, baby." My God, this felt so real because those words are the same verbiage that she would use on earth when I was little girl.

God showed me heaven both times I was hospitalized. This was the symbolism of "hospitalization." I walked into heaven and all my family members that had passed away were there to greet me with their young faces. No one in heaven was old. They were celebrating the coming of a new family member. Suddenly, I came back to reality on my hospital bed and noticed it was only other patients, hospital workers, and doctors before me. I wish I could go back to that moment in time.

God had a different agenda. I was at each place for a reason, so that when my life's plan was revealed, I could look back and say, "That's makes perfect sense." These moments were not coincidental. It shows you that each major life moment symbolizes a particular part of his-story for your life, because your destiny is in the making. He said, "I gave you a glimpse of what heaven looks like." But you can't make it to heaven until you accomplish my assignment here on earth. He took me to those hospitals for a reason. Heaven is the reward after your hard work and dedication for the seed he has planted. This is my destiny in poetic form:

Most people say
She speaks of God too much
She can't speak
Without discussing his name
But why be shame?

I just recognize,
The root of my success
I must let the Holy Ghost,
Speak through my lips of life
Something that most,
Can't relate to.

Understanding the need
Growing the seed,
Producing his deed.

The fire in my eyes,
Power in my feet,
The waves through my hands,

Makes the world turn gold,
My presence before you
Make look bold
And noticeable everywhere we go.

He speaks through my inner voice
And the trio was my choice
I chose them,
They chose me
To fulfill a life of a higher calling.

CHAPTER 16

BRIGHT LIGHTS

Looking out the window, I was staring at the lives of other bullied children that have had similar bullying experiences. We were all considered outcasts amongst peers, left at the lunch table all alone, and treated differently at school. Friends turned their backs on us because we didn't associate with the popular crowd, passed judgment against us because we didn't look like the average person, and used other reasons that go beyond the obvious to alienate us. God made all human beings different but made *truly* bullied children very different. Why is that so? We are separated from the rest because we are the best. Jesus is the only perfect person to have ever existed, and yet he was bullied so passionately by his enemies. They wanted him dead, beat him brutally, and weren't going to sleep until he was crucified on the cross.

Truly bullied children have a quality in common with Jesus. Everywhere he went, his light shined so brightly that it overshadowed his enemies' light. He was charismatic and people were drawn to him like a magnet. Charisma is a quality of an individual of virtue who is set apart from ordinary people and endowed with supernatural, superhuman, and exceptional powers.

I never understood why I would get so much attention from people in public places or have family members excited to see me, classmates thrilled to see me walk in the classroom, and teachers saying, "You are a sweetheart." The signs were obvious, but I was unaware of what God had instilled on the inside. After conversations with strangers, they would see me again and tell me what an amazing person I was, how I truly inspired them with my drive and charisma. It was like a bell being rung at the same time every day. You ignore the ringer and move on to your next goal. I was excited to walk in the classroom and learn something new every day.

Now, I can imagine why I was chosen as a target. I was a little girl who looked like a tomboy, with two black eyes and scars on my face. They called me "Scarface" and "Tina the Termite." It wasn't the external traits but the internal traits that were threatening to the bullies. They figured that if they could degrade my name, then I wouldn't have the willpower to outshine their qualities. Unlike most students, I wasn't trying to get in the popular spotlight. I was content with going to school, making friends naturally, and playing basketball, which was my passion. Through it all, I was a happy school kid and fit in wherever I wanted to be. Loving myself was one of the best decisions I could have made. Friends felt a need to be around me because I was authentic.

Parents will begin to realize that their child was blessed with an unforgettable quality. This quality is magnetic and shines like a star in the sky. You walk in a classroom, all eyes are glued. You go to the playground, kids gather around you to play with you. Everywhere you go, people are fascinated by your charismatic spirit. Not everyone has this gift. Your bullies are the first to detect your qualities in a negative light. They smell your mysterious magnetism.

They say opposites attract, right? The bullied child is the star in this race. Your bullies are the rats. The word *star* spelled backwards is *rats*. Rats are frequently blamed for damaging goods or spreading diseases. Describing a person as *rat-like* usually implies he or she is unattractive and suspicious. Bullies try to damage a child's superior status and make him or her feel like he or she is worthless.

The star will face many rats throughout this race. My bullies came at me in many phases and different angles. They had one motive in mind and that was to degrade the star by all means. These rats build their success off your failures. You must remain in control of your destiny, or it can be diminished if they can destroy your self-esteem. Throughout your life's journey, if your esteem is destroyed, you won't have the desire to function or the will to succeed or follow through with God's destiny for your life.

Bullies choose their victims wisely. They pick on students but target the ones with the smell of stardom. Opposites do attract. Bullies lack strong family unity, physical happiness, high self-esteem, social happiness, and peer acceptance. In my case, my family was unified and I was physically and socially happy. My dad told me frequently to get out of the mirror. I always had high self-esteem and peers accepted me. Friends wanted to be included in my inner circle. It was the bullies and bystanders that laughed, made fun of me, and tried to make me feel like an outcast. I didn't let them depreciate my self-worth because God appreciated my daily walk of life. He made me feel like a million dollars, that I had hit the jackpot and advertised my ticket. I was God's star on his red carpet. I was born a star. Stardom comes with having superior status.

I've spoken with many people today that were affected by being bullied as a child, and they all feel defeated, even as adults. My perception of the conversations was that they actually believed what the bullies said about them. Well, if they said that I will never be anything, then I won't prosper in life and become the star that I was born to be.

Teresa, an adult still affected by bullying as a child, e-mailed me one day on Facebook and told me she was proud of my accomplishments, that I never let anyone get in the way of my success, and that I overcame the bullying. Since she was thirty-one, she felt it was too late for her to succeed. Sincerely, I responded by saying, "Teresa, you shouldn't feel that way. It is never too late to turn your life around."

She said, "I always had dreams and aspirations but was let down by bullies calling me ugly, horrible names."

I said, "It's never too late, and don't let them get the best of you."

She quickly responded by saying, "I am too old to accomplish my dreams and fear of being talked about again and fear the worst."

I pray for her and hope that she can find destiny and hear God's voice. When you are distracted by evil bullies, it can overwhelm you and cause a detour on the road to the success. This is an example of how one student can be affected the rest of his or her future if the foundation is not built within. High self-esteem will carry you very far in life, and I am afraid that children today are not being taught the importance of success by their parents. Teresa's just one of example of how sometimes you never overcome the challenge of being bullied nearly to death. Although she's still alive, she walks around with the grudge weighing heavily, affecting her day-to-day abilities to be more successful. But some students are so affected by bullying that they take their own lives.

Phoebe Prince was charismatic, beautiful, intelligent, and gregarious according to her mother's statement. This case of bullying led to death because her boyfriend's ex-girlfriend tortured her by bullying. Her bullies later apologized, saying that it was their jealously, anger, and hurt that made them say harsh, cruel words to Phoebe. Some reports say she was bullied to death because of all the attention she received from male students. Many were really envious of her and the beauty that God blessed her with. Her bullied name was "Irish whore." Other close friends at South Hadley High said she would have gone to great lengths to make someone else happy.

I read through this story of Phoebe and realized that this was just the breaking point of her bullying era because, before experiencing bullying at South Hadley, she was exposed to it in Ireland. Her aunt allegedly warned school officials, in August 2009, prior to Prince's enrollment at the school, to watch over Phoebe because she was "susceptible" to bullying and was bullied in Ireland. On January 14, 2010, after a day of harassment and taunting, followed by a final incident in which a student threw a can at her from a passing car as she walked home from school, she committed suicide by hanging herself in the stairwell leading to the second floor of her family's apartment.

God revealed to me in 2010, at the time of writing part one of *Diary of a Bullied Child,* that a *truly* bullied child will be a target of bullies everywhere he or she goes. This child can transfer to two or more schools and still will suffer at the hand of bullies. There is no way out of darkness, unless you follow this successful strategy. My success against bullies was the benchmark set for the fight against bullies. You must build a relationship with God, build your self-esteem, focus on God's talent for your life, and never provoke your bullies, if they throw a verbal threat, walk away with a smile; only fight back when you are physically attacked. Never believe what the bullies say.

Your bright light will shine in every school you attend and will make you susceptible to bullying. I didn't make my parents aware for many reasons, one being that I didn't want them to transfer me to another school. Although the bullying acts were ongoing, I felt that I had to face my fears and not run from them. Many parents are devastated that their child will suffer with depression, and they will constantly transfer their children to many different schools. Hopefully, after reading this book, they will realize that God is speaking through my writing and be informed to keep their children within their own school system.

If you teach your children the concepts I previously mentioned, they will defeat their bullies. Now, if they are receiving death threats, email the school system in writing and physically meet with officials. This will show that you have attempted to contact the school. If the school fails to act, then they should be held accountable to the full extent of the law, and your children may have to be homeschooled to avoid further distress and emotional/physical abuse.

Are you a fifth grader? Hello, bright light! This is a time most bullying acts will begin. At the age of ten, God's gift of charisma and ambition will slowly blossom like a beautiful flower. Watch out, because over time you will become the star you were called to be. These children will most definitely be susceptible to bullying because they are chosen to be future leaders. There is nothing wrong with bullied children, and we are blessed to be different because God has made us this way. We were blessed, and our bullies detect our smell of stardom. Our bullies are walking a thin line between love and hate. What must our bullies do to achieve our level of success?

CHAPTER 17

NO WAY OUT OF DARKNESS

Whether bullied children are male or female, they will be attacked by both sexes. You would think that as a young girl I would only fight other little girls. Unfortunately, that wasn't the case. My bullies were both boys and girls. They all smelled the stardom in the air as I walked in the room.

The bully may feel that the only way out is to degrade someone else's character. It's such a lonely place to be when you look in the mirror every day and don't feel accepted by your classmates or don't get the attention you deserve by teachers because you don't look a certain way, or maybe you have accepted yourself but don't fit in socially. You feel the only way to gain that power back is to unleash your unhappiness on another student.

Nowadays, bullies have so much hate for their victims, as if Satan's walking with them daily. Most of them would take pride in the victim's loss of life (by committing suicide). It has been reported cases, bullies have forced victims to practice committing suicide.

Just like Jesus' enemies—they wanted him dead by any means necessary. At times, the bullied child questions, "What could I have done that is so cruel, when I go to school to better myself?"

Some bullies would go to far lengths to make you feel like an outcast at school because you simply just don't fit in. They will hit you on the head with poles and bats, knock you down, shove papers in your face, throw your lunch away, attack you from behind, talk to you with lack of respect, spit in your face, throw you over fences, shove your head in a commode, pull your hair, throw your belongings out of your lockers, and for what reason? The bullied child would like to go to school for educational purposes but is distracted by bullies.

Bullies have a negative fascination with your stardom, and there is no way out of darkness for the bully until you are out of their picture frame. When they wake up, their motivation is you. There is no way out of darkness because they feel the only way out of "hell" is to succeed off others' failures. In order for their mental condition to improve, one must seek counsel from a school official or a parent. It is quite obvious that the bully is far from God's foundation of love. Bullies carry an indicative mood around daily once they detect their target. Once they have teased thirty different students and detected that one target, they are motivated from that point on. If they can defeat you, there is light at the end of their tunnel.

During my era, the bullies didn't see any light. I gave them enough to hang themselves.

They were stuck at the end of a bottomless pit and continued to call on the name of Satan to find another plan of attack. Each plan failed, as I went on to graduate from high school, holding my diploma with sincere gratitude. It was a high honor to know that I had made it that far and that God wasn't going to let me down. He made a promise that he would get me through this battle, if only I continued to have faith as small as a mustard seed.

Some of my main bullies' purpose of attending school was "Tina the Termite." How could they focus on class when I was the target? Wonder what their grades were on their report cards? Do the parents review their grades every six weeks and notice a trend? A trend of inconsistencies and grades fluctuating up and down? If your child is learning in class, then report cards will reflect a consistent pattern of successful grades.

With the ambition and willpower instilled on the inside, the bullied child will have more of an honor-roll pattern, and the bully will typically be an average student or worse. Their focus factor is you, and they couldn't care less about graduating, or if they graduate, it is borderline. As of today, only three of my bullies graduated from high school. Most of them dropped out before making it into junior year of high school and became a part of the failing statistics. So, I conducted my own poll, and I was amazed at the final revelation. The results are that most of my bullies became prisoners and cellmates in jail, walking the streets and selling drugs because that's the route they were limited to. These "average" people can't make it in the modern world. If you live your life from the fifth grade to junior year in high school trying to set a trap for other innocent students, you then become a victim of your own failures.

Bullies can change their evil ways by getting on their knees and repenting before God. Also, they should ask God to rebuke the demons that Satan has on their lives. One must be sincere in doing so. Otherwise, they will forever live a life in regret and denial and have an invisible number written on their foreheads. This number is the daily headcount of prison guards matching your cell to your body.

There is no way out of darkness if you don't first realize that your actions are understood to be devilish. Second, once you have come to the realization that you have been thinking selfishly, you must go before the bullied child and apologize. Sincere apologies are recognized in the eyes of the Lord. Your name will remain in the book of life. Allowing yourself to continue to target "God stars" and tempt them to a level of suicide will cause Satan to gain control of your soul. It will then be lost, and Satan's main goal is to blind you from seeing the kingdom of God. It goes deeper than the day-to-day operations within the school environment to the seed that you plant for your future.

You reap what you sow! If you allow yourself to go to school and gain more knowledge about life, history, reasons why we exist, and the history between God and Satan, then you will understand the reasons why bullying is unhealthy for mankind.

What route will you choose? I hear the sound of the clock ticking. Your decision now to change your thought pattern could be the best road you will ever take. We have to see a clearer picture than just ourselves and review the matter in a more spiritual light. Some people don't believe in a higher power; I know my God is real from my ten years of being bullied. It took his almighty grace to save me from all the fights as "Miss Mike Tyson," "Tina the Scarface," and "Tina the Termite."

Technology has really changed during the twenty-first century. Bullies have more tools at their disposal. They have social media websites to hide behind if they are afraid to tell their targets in person. Posting threats to walls for others to see and sending massive emails to mutual friends are what changed the game of bullying. You have more cases of cyber-bullying. Back in the day, these options weren't available.

In the earlier days, you were just taunted by classmates or teachers face to face. One little girl named Susan would get beaten and bullied as a child every day at school. Negative treatment by others really made her feel bad and caused her to have low self-esteem. On one hand, she was brutally beaten with a belt by teachers. Other days, Susan would get called ugly names by classmates. Her mental disability was the reason teachers would beat her.

Another student, Clay, was verbally abused by classmates all through elementary school and part of junior high. His mother thought it was a bit of a mystery because she didn't understand why her son was chosen by bullies. His school days were so tough that he didn't want to go to school. He found a passion for singing at school when he was young. The bullies' motivation was Clay, and he thought he was picked on because he found some enjoyment in singing.

Isolated student Stefani was bullied and picked on because of her rabbit teeth and big nose. She was made fun of often and bullies threw her in the trash can. They wanted her to feel worthless. Her bullies told her she was a loser and would never be anything. Stefani had a really good relationship with her father that helped her through her lonely road to acceptance.

CHAPTER 18

BULLYING ERA

I woke up many days in the hospital with angels dropping clue after clue about an unfamiliar term called "bull fever." The angels from heaven stopped by and said, "You will walk with honor, as your bullies will choose you as a donor." Suddenly another clue unfolded right before my eyes. Your temperature will rise and reach an all-time high with pokes of a deadly needle infected with the serious disease of getting bullied. After each poke, whether it's the name-calling, getting pushed, being shoved into the lockers, or getting hit on the head with a pole, my mind blacked out from the unexpected damage to the brain. The verbal, mental, and physical abuse left me wounded in no man's land, wondering why I was chosen as a target.

How could I have recovered from such harsh criticism? After a couple days, I reached for a star in the sky to shed some light on an illness my body seemed to fight. I was okay after each incident for only a couple of days. I was asking God why my name was on the bullies' donor list of fame. I was hot like fire, and they added fuel to my flame. They later became my motivation. Every day, I wore the armor of my higher power, and my body was cleansed by a shower from my evil bullies. After the cleansing, I looked in the mirror and thought to myself, "The needle shots' short-term pain didn't faze me." The angel showed me that the bull is allergic to the color red, and I was the future star on God's red carpet. The angel from heaven showed me that there is a process that God's stars will go through before the hidden secret is revealed—that they are the future stars within their generations.

Once the realization becomes reality, the bullying acts won't even matter to you, and it will suddenly come to a close. Then the bullied can rise to destiny, to a life of a higher calling to lead their generations to change, prosperity, creativity, and inspiration. The bully rats were allergic to the "star" medicine, which was star power and fame. I was chosen by God to shed some light on the real reason we are chosen by our bullies and to keep the future generations from developing low self-esteem, suffering depression, committing suicide, or targeting others because they are bullied. It is not just a rite of passage. Bullying has been occurring for many centuries, and pundits have never understood the root of the matter. We have been saved by the best doctor to have ever existed. Now, we can look back over our journeys and make a pathway to our future destinations.

In most cases, the bullying era is over once the bullied child leaves high school and moves away from the people that made it hell on earth during school days. High school graduation takes forever to come because you look at the clock as it slowly ticks.

The end of the bullying era came to a closure for Susan, Clay, and Stefani after their high school years, but the aftermath added up to a gain of personal freedom as they said their goodbyes to their bullies. Looking back, they all feel the dramatic weight on their hearts as they struggle to find themselves after all the negativity endured over the years. Susan once contemplated suicide but later realized that there was a reward waiting in leftfield if she endured the fight.

CHAPTER 19
YOU GOT TALENT

The reward that had Susan's name on it was an accomplishment worth waiting for.

After walking out on stage, she realized the struggles had begun to pay off. Her payoff was worth millions of dollars, as if she had hit the jackpot. Susan always knew she could sing and often turned to her voice for escape. Singing was her passion. She had a voice that superseded her adversaries. Susan Boyle was destined to become a superstar. Her name was in a drawing on her birthdate and that changed the hands of time. All of her battles, nights in tears, and beatings from her peers and teachers prepared her for the biggest stage, *Britain's Got Talent.* Right before her eyes, her nightmares sensationally became her greatest dreams. She saw a crowd full of fans showing an unbelievable amount of support she never had seen before. Susan could always sing, but God waited for the right place and right time. When she turned forty-eight years old, it was her time to shine. Her first album, entitled *I Dreamed a Dream,* became Amazon's greatest selling album in presales three months before its release date.

In Britain, her album was recognized as the fastest selling UK album of all time. Susan's rapid rise to fame seemed to have happened overnight, but this was predestined to exist.

Her bullies named her "Susie Simple" at school, but it had been changed to "Susie the Superstar." The devil meant it for bad, but

God meant it for good. Susan has become a role model for anyone with a dream.

Bullies hit her on the head, burned her clothes, and psychologically hurt her with the constant name-calling. She felt no one loved her and didn't know why she was a target. Picked on relentlessly because she had a disability? Susan never realized that she felt different for a reason. She was a "destiny child."

Although you are chosen to be a superstar, your time to shine in front of cameras won't be until God reveals your name on the red carpet. The red carpet is where the stars shine and their bullies are blinded by their stardom.

Clay Aiken has been revealed as another star on the red carpet. His story of bullying was inspirational to many. He went to school for a purpose, and harassing other students wasn't one of them. After graduating from school, Clay later became one of America's success stories. Singing on *American Idol,* Clay won the hearts of many fans, and although he came in second place, the road to stardom went straight through the green light to Hollywood. It opened many avenues for his career as an actor, author, and songwriter. His first album, *Measure of Man,* debuted in first place on the *Billboard* 200 and became the highest selling debut for a solo artist in ten years.

His friends were rich and had everything, so why would they pick on him? What did they have to gain from picking on a little boy that had a passion to sing and do high school musicals? The angel flew across Clay's bathroom mirror and shouted "Bull fever!" Many stars never realized what the term meant. He had many sleepless nights because he was afraid to go to sleep, thinking the bullies would attack him in his dreams.

Another angel whispered, "You're chosen." Hollywood only grows as the stars grow. Hollywood is your heaven on earth. You must conquer school days before you receive the Survivor of the Years award. If you noticed, that it is *years* instead of *year.* This battle will go on for numerous years because of who you were born to be.

I opened my eyes from a deep dream, and there was a rainbow in the sky. As I stared at it for a while, the yellow in the rainbow had the name *Gaga* on it. The angel mentioned Lady Gaga. In my mental notes there was a little girl by the name of Stefani that was bullied relentlessly for having rabbit teeth. She always felt like a freak in school because she didn't think she fit in. During her days, she felt a need to laugh with the bullies to keep from crying.

After she rose to stardom, I listened to her stories as she shared them with the world. To this day, she is still bruised from name-calling and not in her comfort zone unless she's on stage singing. Bullying has left her in the rain with no umbrella. She has no self-acceptance but often gets a boost of pride when her concerts sell out and fans scream her name. Overall, happiness only comes from within oneself, and looking for love onstage will leave a void that can't ever be fulfilled offstage.

Stefani hated going to school and would get teased for being ugly, for the way she wore her makeup, for her big ears, and for her passion to always sing. Little boys threw her in the garbage can. They called her really ugly names in front of huge crowds, and her grades suffered from the humiliation. She was at one point a straight-*A* student and was ashamed of who she was. Bullies mercilessly bullied her for being different. Those were the characteristics many might argue on the enemies' behalf, but was stardom and fame rooted on the inside of her temple? Was stardom invisible when she was school-aged?

Gaga started to take her singing talent to the next level. Suddenly, after numerous club performances, she caught the eye of Akon, another performer and producer, and that is how she found the pathway to destiny. The right place at the right time. She started her career in singing at the age of nineteen but later was signed by Akon's label and became an instant success. Her first album, *The Fame*, hit the number one charts in Australia, Sweden, and Canada. The album sold over fifteen million copies worldwide. The superstar was blessed with the flavor of success and became a force to be reckoned with. Her earlier years in shame fueled her passion to worldwide superstardom. She was the first to make history with four number one hits from a debut album.

"Michael, Michael, Michael," the angel whispered in my ear. Who might this be? It was a rising star with plenty of passion and talent to spread across the skies. He was hot like fire and became a sensation overnight.

In 2008, Michael Phelps earned worldwide respect for his performance at the Beijing Olympic Games, as he earned the title of greatest Olympian ever with his record for most individual Olympic gold medals, a total of nine. And although he has been called "amazing," "incredible," and even "Sportsman of the Year," Phelps was branded with much different terms as a kid. He was taunted for his "sticky-out ears" and lisp, as well as his long arms, which ultimately took him to greatness. It seems that the taunting Phelps experienced encouraged his greatness, with coach Bob Bowman reporting, "Michael is the motivation machine—bad moods, good moods, he channels everything for gain." Including, we presume, childhood taunting. Phelps is apparently able to take any adversity and turn it into a reason to train harder, going so far as to train during Christmas. His story is one of particular inspiration to bullied kids everywhere, showing that you can not only survive taunting but turn it into motivation to be amazing.

The game is a tough play but winning is a sweet success. We will face many struggles, but our greatest strength, in the midst of bullying, is our talent. Whether it is singing, dancing, writing, swimming, modeling, acting, golfing, comedy, or basketball, these will turn our pain into passion. Your life will be driven by your desires and fueled by the enemies mind games that try to create self-doubt. When the devil throws the curve ball, you dodge it by the concentration on what makes you happy. You ignore the voices and make the choices to fulfill your dreams because you realize that you have found destiny. After traveling the journey of high school, you discover destiny and make it possible to achieve the impossible. You will walk on the highest stage in life because that was God's plan. You must grind through the valleys before you enjoy the winds that blow on the mountaintops. America will have a superstar to lead and inspire the new generations. In order to be a fearless advocate, you must have been a survivor yourself.

Every dream, vision, and thought from God about your destiny is his way of slowly rolling out the red carpet. Listen to no one else, for his voice outweighs the sighs from family members, friends, and coworkers. These people will push you away from his plan for your life, leaving you to settle for less. The outcasts have become America's heavyweights in their field of talents. Superstars own the stage they walk on and are now known as destiny children.

CHAPTER 20

THE SINGER

L et your voice be heard. Put your feelings into writing. As a bullied child, that is exactly what Taylor Swift experienced. The mean-girl club attacked her daily, and she felt miserable and was afraid to attend school. At the very young age of eight, she found her talent in writing, and in moments of distress, pen and paper were her best friends. Writing music inspired her to conquer this fight and not let her bullies label her.

Bullies didn't think she was pretty enough to associate with them and were really mean to her on purpose, which caused Taylor to have low self-esteem. They would have parties and exclude her name from the invitation list. During the week, friends would gather and tease her for not being invited to the weekend festivities. She was alone most of her school days because no one accepted her. There were days that she would sit at the lunch table with friends and they would leave the table. People thought she was weird and felt a need to stay far away from her. Oh, really! Was she that weird, or could it have been the fresh smell of stardom?

Taylor was content with the bullying after a while because she would just write a song about it later. One of her hit songs, "Mean," is an anthem that recognizes bullying and won her two Grammys for best country song and best solo country performance. Her second album, entitled *Fearless,* attracted a wide audience and became the top-selling album of 2009. The record won her four

Grammy awards, and she became the youngest ever Album of the Year winner. Swift's third album, *Speak Now,* sold over one million copies in its first week.

I awoke from a deep dream and looked up at the ceiling. There were three angels dancing around me and singing a song called "You Got Bull Fever, You Got Bull Fever." I shook my head and said, "Do you mean I got bull fever?" Yes, but the singer Rihanna has been diagnosed with bull fever this time around. Many patients will leave the doctor's office with surprising results. So, there it goes. Another name revealed as they drop clue after clue. The singer Rihanna had bull fever and has recovered from the symptoms of this epidemic. The fever is contagious with the right germ, called stardom.

Rihanna faced many bullies in her school days. They taunted her for being light-skinned. They teased her over and over again because she was a Barbadian girl that appeared to be white. Students would curse her out, and it left the star really confused. The harassment continued all the way until her last day in elementary school.

She found her path to destiny and became a superstar within the music industry and a leader in the digital world. *Billboard* named Rihanna the highest selling digital artist in US history, having sold 47,571,000 singles. Since the beginning of her singing career, she has sold 25 million albums.

Roll out the red carpet for another superb star in the industry that continues to captivate the world with her superior status—drum roll please!—Christina Aguilera! Bullies hated her for her profound success in her earlier days. She auditioned at the age of twelve for the Mickey Mouse Club and won the part, until the show ended. Dreams of becoming a singer had the superstar on a mission to fulfill destiny. After starring in the Mickey Mouse Club and several talent shows, it drove her bullies insane. They tried to slash her mother's tires if she won a certain competition. Her life seemed perfect on stage, but offstage it was a nightmare and a hell full of bullies.

Christina's mother admits the tactics of jealous school kids often went beyond the schoolyards and into the talent shows. She explains,

"We would have to watch her equipment—the school's equipment—because when it was Christine's turn to perform, her bullies would unplug her equipment."

By the sixth grade, she was having nightmares. It was so crazy that the superstar had to get therapy treatment. Feeling confused and miserable, she said she had to get out of school and go get her dream outside of school. She then found other friends, like this little boy named Justin Timberlake and a little girl named Britney Spears. "It felt so good to find that support system," quoted the superstar. She was known locally as the little girl with a big voice.

Today, she is a worldwide superstar and was born to win. Her debut album, *Christina Aguilera,* was a commercial success with three number one hits on the *Billboard* Hot 100. She was recognized for her vocal ability, music videos, and image, all of which gained her a spot on the Hollywood Walk of Fame and earned her four Grammy awards.

It was five o'clock, and the bell started to ring. This was a sign that it was time for more revelation. Looking at the clock, it appeared to have Demi's name written all over it. Though time is of the essence, there is no time to be wasted as I complete a journey of names revealed on the red carpet of stardom.

Demi Lovato was tormented in school for being fat and alone. The bullies made her feel helpless, and often she would cry, telling her mom that she didn't want to go to school anymore. She had an unhealthy relationship with food since the age of eight because of the bullying, and she began self-mutilating her wrists to cope with the pain, until the age of eleven. Her bullied name was "ugly whore." Bullies often called her ugly. Demi believed what the bullies were saying and took the cruel words to heart. She thought the reason she didn't have friends was because she was fat. So, she starved herself and vomited up anything she did eat. Her pain was felt so deeply that she threw up six times a day. The final straw was when she was chased into the toilets by other girls who were threatening to punch her. At thirteen, she quit school to escape her bullies and became homeschooled with her new friend, Selena Gomez. While being homeschooled, she was able to focus on her career and was inspired to write music. Now, she is still traumatized by the cruel treatment and wonders if the scars will ever heal.

Demi is a known actress as well as a prominent singer. She starred in *Barney & Friends, Camp Rock, Sonny with a Chance,* and *Princess Protection Program.* She also released her debut album, *Don't Forget,* and it was number two on the *Billboard* 200, selling eighty-nine thousand copies in the first week. It had then shipped over five hundred thousand copies, earning a gold certificate in the United States. The second album, *Here We Go Again,* debuted at number one on the *Billboard* 200, selling one hundred and eight thousand in its first week. Album number three, *Unbroken,* was number four on the charts.

This next bullied child will not only knock the socks off your feet but will have you in a state of shock. You will wonder no more why he was a prime target of bullies. His lyrics will begin to sound a little different than the other stars. Eminem was reportedly bullied so badly at the age of nine that his mother ended up suing! There are records to show that he suffered from cerebral concussion, post-traumatic headaches, intermittent loss of vision and hearing, and other injuries to his head, face, back, and neck. Bullies treated him so badly that he also suffered with nightmares and anti-social behavior. During one fight with a bully, his lip was split and he almost got the wind knocked out of him.

Eminem was so affected by the bullying acts that he had to switch school many times, but he realized that it only made it worst and later dropped out of school at the age of seventeen, after repeating the ninth grade twice. Being the new kid on the block, he was pushed into lockers and beat up in hallways and bathrooms. Later, he found a dose of passion and began to write music and lyrics to songs that became hits down the road. Talent gave the superstar confidence and inspired him to become a storyteller.

The bullies added fuel to his fire. Eminem was not only one of the best-selling artists of all time but *the* best selling artist of the 2000s. He has sold more than 42 million tracks and 41.5 million albums in the United States and nearly 90 million albums worldwide. His superstar status became noticeable in 1999 with his debut album, *The Slim Shady LP*. Also, with his third album, *The Eminem Show*, he received Grammy awards, making Eminem the first ever artist to receive Best Rap Album for three consecutive LPs. Under his heavyweight belt, he has earned thirteen Grammy awards.

As you can see, those rats that try to damage the goods of the destiny children often sit back and witness the flavor of success within the stars' future careers, topping the *Billboard* charts, Olympic podiums, and other worldwide stages. Although they moved on to fulfill a life that was predestined for them, sometimes stars are sidetracked by the bullying that crippled them in their earlier days, leaving them with no cane to walk on, a bridge to fall off of, stomachs that felt so empty, heads grinding with constant pain, and no one to understand their struggles. The children of destiny found a way out of the jungle. Only the strongest will endure life, pass the jungle, and become survivors.

CHAPTER 21
THE MODEL

Look in the mirror and tell me what you see. Beauty beyond the bullying isn't what models were teased for. Many of today's top models played the role of ugly-duckling-turned-swan. Although it's hard to believe, some have been bullied for being tall and skinny or for having distinctive features that later became the ticket to superstardom on the runway. Lindsey Wixson, a seventeen-year-old model, quickly rose to fame due to her gap-toothed smile, full lips, and baby doll face. She said, "I was actually self-conscious about my gap." In middle school, a group of girls was always trying to beat her up and called her gap a "parking lot." She said it was the worst time of her life. Modeling has really built her self-confidence, and she has made a successful destiny as a glamorous model.

She mentioned to the group of bullies that she was looking for a modeling agent at the lunch table, and they came back a week later with a list of things they didn't like about her. By the age of sixteen, she dropped out of school, but she later took the GED to receive her diploma.

Tyra Banks felt like a freak at school. The bullies made her life a living hell. They teased her relentlessly about being tall and skinny. Her bullied stage name was "Olive Oyl." She used to break down and cry because no one wanted to sit by her in class. One little boy stated, "I don't want to sit by a tall, skinny, braces-wired mouth, big-forehead girl anymore." She was in tears from all the comments made about her looks, and she was emotionally weak. Other names were given to her, too, such as "Light-bulb head" and "Five-head."

She later became a superstar model for *Sports Illustrated, Vogue,* Pepsi, Nike, Tommy Hilfiger, Ralph Lauren, and McDonalds. Strutting her thin frame down the runway, Tyra is now one of the wealthiest supermodels in history.

Supermodel Chanel Iman rose to fame overnight for her beauty. She said she was always bullied for being skinny and tall her whole life. Early on, she listened to others and failed to appreciate what God gave her until "I at least accepted what an amazing blessing it was to love me for me," quoted the superstar.

Eva Mendes is one of Hollywood's leading covergirl, but as a young girl, she suffered attacks from bullies. She explains, "I was a gawky, skinny girl with big teeth and that made me an easy target. I had two bullies, and they tortured me all through junior high school." And although they made her miserable at school, eventually she found the courage she needed to push back against them. "Only later could I see that I was showing them my fear and that's what they were pouncing on." Mendes recalls, "When I finally stood up to my bully, that's when things changed for me," and she encourages those who are being bullied to stand up for themselves as well. Although Mendes is proud that she showed courage and fought back against her bullies, she does think they left their mark: "I'm sure those experiences explain why I've been so anxiety-ridden in my adult life."

As a celebrated Hollywood sex symbol, it's hard to believe an unattractive, bullied Jessica Alba growing up. But the star insists that it's true and that she had a terrible time fitting in at school. Her family didn't have as much money as others in her class and she had a Texan accent and buck teeth. She was deemed uncool and frequently attacked for being different. Alba spent her lunches in the nurses' office for solitude and safety, and her dad had to walk her to school so that she wouldn't be provoked. She never fought back, not wanting to lower herself to the level of her bullies, but she did find an outlet for her frustration and fear: acting classes. Alba recalls, "The idea that for an hour I could be someone different was amazing. I was determined that this was something I was going to be good at. This was a part of my life no bully could ruin." She says that her lessons at drama school "changed everything" and sparked a lifelong love of acting. Alba encourages others who have been bullied to use fear as fuel: "You have to make it push you to become a stronger person, in whatever way that may be."

It's hard to feel sorry for people as pretty as Megan Fox, but it's comforting that she also endured high school harassment. She says, "I was bullied and it's hard; you feel like high school's never going to be over. It's four years of your life, and you just have to remember the person picking on you had their own problems and their own issues. And you're going to be okay . . . usually bullies are the most insecure." Doesn't it seem like high school was way longer than four years?

CHAPTER 22

THE GOLFER & THE COMEDIAN

On Tiger Woods' first day of kindergarten in 1981, the future golf stud was tied to a tree and taunted with racial slurs by older schoolboys. While that incident seems to be the only one of such a level of severity, Woods was an impressive student who didn't let others bring him down. He garnered mostly A's in school and then went on to study at Stanford University. He has been credited with inspiring the interests of other minorities, and youth in general, in the name of golf. Ever since he was three, his profound love for golf has translated into more PGA wins than any other golfer. In 2006, Woods was named *Forbes* highest paid athlete and ranks second on the list of overall paid celebrities, making around $87 million a year.

He had the eye of a tiger since birth, but at the age of three, he shot a forty-eight over nine holes at the Navy Golf Course, and at the age of five, he appeared in *Golf Digest* with additional appearances on ABC's *That's Incredible*. Tiger's smell of stardom started to permeate the airwaves way before most stars, the reason he was attacked by older bullies. With him being so young, it was impossible for him to comprehend what was happening.

Neither did Chris Rock have a clue that he was wearing the sweet smell of stardom. He was walking around school getting beat up by bullies and being called a nigger every single day. The fights were so bad that his parents had to have him bused to schools in predominately white neighborhoods of Brooklyn, New York. As he got older, the bullying got worse, and his parents decided to pull him out of James Madison High School. He thought it would be better to drop out of school and pursue his GED.

Rock began doing stand-up comedy in 1984 in New York City's Catch a Rising Star. He slowly rose up the ranks of the comedy circuit and earned bit roles in the film *I'm Gonna Git You Sucka* and the TV series *Miami Vice*. Upon seeing his act at a nightclub, Eddie Murphy befriended and mentored the aspiring comic. Murphy gave Rock his first film role in *Beverly Hills Cop II*.

He later had two HBO comedy specials: *Bigger & Blacker* in 1999, and *Never Scared* in 2004. Articles relating to both specials called Rock "the funniest man in America" in *Time* and *Entertainment Weekly*. HBO also aired his talk show, *The Chris Rock Show*, which gained critical acclaim for Rock's interviews with celebrities and politicians. The show won an Emmy for writing. His television work has won him a total of three Emmy awards and fifteen nominations. By the end of the decade, Rock was established as one of the preeminent stand-up comedians and comic minds of his generation. His fifth HBO special, *Kill the Messenger*, won him another Emmy for outstanding writing for a variety or music program.

Chris turned his pain into passion with the hit TV true-to-life sitcom, *Everybody Hates Chris*. Not everyone gets an outlet like TV to share their bullying experiences, but Rock has benefited from the show: one of his former teachers sent an apology letter to him after seeing the previews, saying, "I knew it was hard on you, but I had no idea. If anything happened to you because of me, please forgive me." The show was based on a bullied child being rejected by his classmates and centered around him getting beat up by bullies because he was black, but in real life, it was who he was born to be a future superstar bound for a major legacy. He has earned his right to superstardom.

CHAPTER 23
THE ACTOR

Tom Cruise, the star of *Top Gun* and *Mission Impossible,* is beloved worldwide for his talent and looks, but as a kid, he wasn't so appreciated. Cruise's childhood was spent on the move, as his father constantly uprooted the family to find a new source of work and support the family. As a result, he had to establish himself over and over again at new schools: "I was always the new kid with the wrong shoes, the wrong accent. I didn't have the friend to share things with and confide in." And at each school, he faced the experience repeatedly. He was small for his age and easily pushed around. Eventually, he learned to stand up for himself, but at every new school, he had to fight over and over again. "Your heart's pounding, you sweat, and you feel like you're going to vomit. I'm not the biggest guy, I never liked hitting someone, but I know if I don't hit that guy hard he's going to pick on me all year. I go, 'You better fight.' I just laid it down. I don't like bullies." Cruise found strength and inspiration in his mother, who he says, "rose to the occasion," supporting the family on her own with three jobs. Once seeing her success, Cruise turned a corner, deciding, "I'm going to create, for myself, who I am, not what other people say I should be."

Christian Bale starred in *Empire of the Sun* when he was thirteen years old, but instead of an instant entourage, he was instantly hated in school. Bale says, "It was not a great time. I was a victim of bullying and had other kids kicking and punching me every day. It was an early lesson in how making a film can set you apart. If you don't want to live with the consequences then don't make the film. But that didn't help at the time. I was confused about other people's reactions to me, both good and bad. It can mess anyone up." I bet they got way nicer once *Newsies* came out and they realized what an awesome singer Christian is!

Chad Michael Murray said, "I had my two front teeth knocked out by a sixth grader in first grade. He picked me up and jacked me in the mouth. My house got egged, and all that stuff that happens to you when you're growing up with people who don't understand what's going on. I hated high school, to be honest. I enjoyed the educational part of it; my teachers allowed me to be creative. But I didn't have any friends because I didn't fit in. I thought past high school to what I wanted to do."

Jackie Chan was bullied when he was a child because he was "too scared" to stand up for himself. Starting his acting career at the age of five, Jackie admits he wasn't so brave and was often picked on by the other children at his school because he was such an easy target. Jackie endured years of torment, only learning to defend himself after he stood up for another child. "I was bullied quite a lot when I was growing up in my Peking Opera School," he explained. "I allowed myself to be bullied because I was scared and didn't know how to defend myself. I was bullied until I prevented a new student from being bullied. By standing up for him, I learned to stand up for myself."

Jackie Chan has received worldwide recognition for his acting, having won several awards, including an Innovator Award from the American Choreography Awards and a lifetime achievement award from the Taurus World Stunt Awards. He has stars on the Hollywood Walk of Fame and the Hong Kong Avenue of Stars.

Kevin Costner was bullied relentlessly; he had to change schools a lot. The fact remains that if you are a star, every school ground that you walk on, regardless of what school you transfer to, you still will be a target. You can't escape the stardom because it is visible everywhere you go. Well, he didn't let his bullies defeat him, as he went on to graduate from high school in 1973 and college in 1978, with his BA in marketing and finance. Later, he found destiny and started his acting career. He has won two Academy awards and two Golden Globes and has been nominated for three BAFTA (British Academy of Film and Television Arts) awards.

An introverted loner in high school, Harrison Ford attended Maine East High School in Park Ridge, Illinois, where he says he was picked on by his peers and voted the boy "least likely to succeed." Ford silently endured the taunting and abuse of his peers until he one day snapped and beat up his aggressors' leader. It wasn't until Ford took a drama class (mainly as a way to meet women) during his junior year at Ripon College in Wisconsin that he became fascinated with acting. While he auditioned for roles on television and in movies, Ford also supported himself as a carpenter, which helped to land him his biggest movie role ever. *Star Wars* series director George Lucas hired Ford to build some cabinets in his home and asked him to read lines with actors rehearsing for *Star Wars IV: A New Hope.* It was Steven Spielberg who first noticed that Ford would make a great Han Solo, and well, the rest is history!

As a teenager, Steven Spielberg's family moved from Phoenix, Arizona, to Saratoga, California. The kids at Saratoga High School picked on Spielberg for being Jewish. It's also suspected that the kids picked on Spielberg because he showed symptoms of Asperger's Syndrome. One symptom related to Asperger's is delay in the development of social skills. When asked about his experiences at Saratoga High School, Spielberg would always say that it was "hell on earth." Nowadays, most people and aspiring filmmakers deem Spielberg's life to be more like "heaven on earth."

CHAPTER 24
THE ACTRESS

Whitney Houston was bullied in school and had memories of being taunted relentlessly over her looks by some girls. They called her ugly, and she suffered from bull fever in her school days. She was a creature according to bullies but later became one of America's best features.

At the early age of eleven, Houston started performing as a soloist in the junior gospel choir at the New Hope Baptist Church in Newark, where she also learned to play the piano. Her first solo performance in the church was "Guide Me, O Thou Great Jehovah." When Houston was a teenager, she attended Mount Saint Dominic Academy, a Catholic girls' high school in Caldwell, New Jersey. While Houston was still in school, her mother continued to teach her how to sing. Houston was also exposed to the music of Chaka Khan, Gladys Knight, and Roberta Flack, most of whom would have an influence on her as a singer and performer.

Houston spent some of her teenage years touring nightclubs where her mother, Cissy, was performing, and she would occasionally get on stage and perform with her. In 1977, at age fourteen, she became a backup singer on the Michael Zager Band's single "Life's a Party." In 1978, at age fifteen, Houston sang background vocals on Chaka Khan's hit single "I'm Every Woman," a song she would later turn into a bigger hit for herself on her monster-selling *The*

Bodyguard soundtrack. She also sang backup on albums by Lou Rawls and Jermaine Jackson.

In the early 1980s, Houston started working as a fashion model after a photographer saw her at Carnegie Hall singing with her mother. She appeared in *Seventeen* and became one of the first women of color to grace the cover of the magazine. She was also featured in layouts in the pages of *Glamour, Cosmopolitan, Young Miss*, and appeared in a Canada Dry soft drink TV commercial. Her striking looks and girl-next-door charm made her one of the most sought-after teen models of that time.

Houston is the only artist to chart seven consecutive number-one *Billboard* Hot 100 hits. She is the second artist behind Elton John and the only female artist to have two number-one *Billboard* 200 album awards (formerly Top Pop Album) on the *Billboard* magazine yearend charts. Houston's 1985 debut album, *Whitney Houston,* became the best-selling debut album by a female act at the time of its release. The album was named *Rolling Stone's* best album of 1986 and was ranked at number 254 on *Rolling Stone's* list of the 500 Greatest Albums of All Time. Her second studio album, *Whitney* (1987), became the first album by a female artist to debut at number one on the *Billboard* 200 albums chart.

At Fountain Valley High School, Michelle Pfeiffer was taunted for having big lips and walking like a duck. These taunts stayed with her through her thirties. She was nicknamed Michelle Mudturtle. The first few times, Michelle admits to having run home crying; however, she eventually became equally violently defensive and a bully in the bargain. She was the biggest in her class and started to handle other people's arguments as well as her own, bashing people frequently—including the boys. Later she spoke about it frankly: "I was a rotten kid, just rotten. If anyone needed anyone beaten up, they would come and get me."

She graduated from high school in 1975 and then won the Miss Orange County beauty pageant in 1978. Later the same year, she participated in Miss California, finishing sixth. Following her participation in these pageants, she acquired an acting agent and began to audition for television and films.

During the 1990s, Pfeiffer attracted comments in the media for her beauty. In 1990, she appeared on the cover of *People* magazine's first "50 Most Beautiful People in the World" issue. She was again featured on the cover of the annual issue in 1999, having made the "Most Beautiful" list a record six times during the decade (1990, 1991, 1992, 1993, 1996, and 1999). Pfeiffer is the first celebrity to have appeared on the cover of the annual issue twice, and the only person to be featured on the cover twice during the 1990s. She received a star on the Hollywood Walk of Fame on August 6, 2007.

Sandra Bullock dreaded school as a kid because she was teased by bullies for wearing frumpy clothes bought in Germany. The actress and her younger sister, Gesine, regularly accompanied their mother, Helga, a German opera singer, as she traveled from their home in Virginia to perform in Europe.

But the constant travel abroad left Bullock clueless as to what was fashionable in her native United States. The star recalls, "I would make the switch on the plane from speaking English to German or vice versa, depending on whichever country we were going to . . . I'd come back (to school) from Europe and I looked like a clown compared to the cool way the other students looked and dressed. So I got my behind whooped a little bit. Kids are mean, and the sad thing is that I can still remember the first and last names of every one of those kids who were mean to me!"

Michelle Trachtenberg is one of those actresses who's not a household name, but after stints as Harriet the Spy, Buffy the Vampire Slayer, and as Georgina Sparks on *Gossip Girl*, she's one of those actresses most people instinctively like. That, apparently, wasn't the case in high school, where she was bullied mercilessly. "This one girl threw me down a flight of stairs, fractured my ribs, punched and fractured my nose, and told the principal I used the word 'bitch' and got me detention." She just recently got revenge when she saw this same woman outside a restaurant where paparazzi were swarming. "They were probably waiting for Paris Hilton, and I just happened to come out," said Michelle. "I have never before or since said something like this, because it's so disgusting, but I turned to her and was like, 'Oh, I'm sorry. I'm really famous. They need to take my picture. Sucks for you.'"

Victoria Beckham says that her life in school wasn't all that posh. "People would push me around, say they were going to beat me up after school, chase me," she said. "It was miserable, my whole schooling, miserable. I tried to be friends with people, but I didn't fit in. So I kept myself to myself."

Although Miley Cyrus seems to be quite popular as a teen, her preteen (and pre-fame) years in Tennessee were a completely different experience. At school, there was an "Anti-Miley Club" full of "big, tough girls" who were "fully capable of doing [her] bodily harm" and went above and beyond in their bullying pursuit. Cyrus was once locked in a bathroom during class: "They shoved me in. I was trapped. I banged on the door until my fists hurt. Nobody came. I spent what felt like an hour in there, waiting for someone to rescue me, wondering how my life had gotten so messed up." Other incidents included challenging Cyrus to a fight, which only ended when the principal stepped in.

And when Cyrus wasn't being physically abused, she was being teased, with classmates telling her, "Your dad's a one-hit wonder. You'll never amount to anything—just like him." Fortunately for her, Cyrus did not listen to naysayers, scoring the role of Hannah Montana and a ticket to fame and fortune.

As one of the most beautiful and talented women in Hollywood, it's hard to believe that anyone would pick on Oscar-winner Kate Winslet about her looks, but it's true. Growing up, Winslet was bullied and teased for being chubby. Her nickname at school was Blubber, and she was once even locked in the art cupboard. And although she is now adored by many worldwide, girls at school told her that no one would ever "fancy" her. Winslet may have grown out of her young awkwardness, but she has not yet shed the painful words of her youth. She says that she still feels like "the fat schoolgirl" and even now doesn't "consider [herself] some kind of great, sexy beauty," acknowledging that magazine covers are retouched, and she's greatly helped in films by hair, makeup, and lighting.

CHAPTER 25

QUEENS BOULEVARD

You have now taken a page turn to Queens Boulevard. There awaits two queens that later became the world's cover girls. They both have something in common, being bullied by rats. Kate Middleton is now married to Princess Diana's son William. The world was graced by her beauty in 2011 when they wed, and the paparazzi had a field day snapping photos of her and the prince. Her savvy style of fashion graced the cover of magazines, but it wasn't so glorifying in her earlier days. Growing up, Kate was known as the ugly duckling. Bullies teased her, threatened her, and made school days miserable. She transferred to several schools, one of which was Downe House. It was reported that she feared going to school because they constantly picked on her for being too skinny and meek, too soft and too nice. It appeared Kate's gangly appearance made her an easy target for classmates. Her parents withdrew her only after being there for two months. This school was costly, at ten thousand a term. The cost didn't stop them from taking her away from the misery.

Kate's bullies smeared her bed with excrement and stole her books and other belongings as a part of a hate campaign against her. When she would go to lunch, she would sit down at the table with people and then others would leave. Her unhappiness was very quiet, but the smell of stardom was very strong at Downe House. Would Kate be where she was today if she hadn't been faced with this despair of pain from bullies? It is certain that bullying helped mold her confidence.

Dana Owens, who later became Queen Latifah, was bullied a lot as a kid for claims that she was gay. Bullies also taunted her because she had big boobs, and they said she was too much of a woman. Now, she graces the fronts of magazines as one of America's leading cover girls. The queen has her own collection for women of color called the Covergirl queen collection. Also, for her outstanding work in film and television, she has received a Golden Globe award and a Grammy award.

Queens Boulevard was designed by architects just for the arrival of the two queens. If they persevered through the bullying, the role of becoming a queen was a part of their destiny. Both ladies were taunted by bullies and added with a dose of self-confidence equals the star equation.

CHAPTER 26

THE PRESIDENTS

The road to the presidency was destined for charismatic Bill Clinton and Barack Obama.

Long before Bill Clinton became our forty-second president, he struggled with self-image and body weight. During his fight against childhood obesity, the former president noted that his love for fast food was a likely contributor to his need for his September 2004 quadruple bypass. "I realized that one more time I've been given another chance, and I wanted to make the most of it," said Clinton. "I was the fat band boy wearing unfashionable jeans." During a YMCA dance, an older boy teased Clinton for donning carpenter's pants. When Clinton jawed back, the boy, who stood a whopping six-foot-six, punched him in the jaw. Clinton may have come out of it with a sore face, but after taking the hit like a champ, standing his ground, and earning the respect of the older student, the politician also gained a lesson in perseverance.

President Obama became our forty-fourth president and was also bullied in his earlier years. Bullies picked on him because he had big ears and because of his name, Barack Hussein Obama. Those words didn't hurt Obama. In fact, he thought what they were saying was senseless, and he was motivated to be the best he could be. He grew up and was ambitious to become a successful leader. After graduating from high school, he was determined to become a lawyer and later went to Harvard University on a scholarship. The long road to destiny didn't stop there, as he went on to being a community organizer and a US senator. The platform had been set. He brought America hope. When he opened his mouth, you could feel change, hope, and the charisma that he was blessed with. As he walked out on the stage to speak, the bright lights were shining brightly. The presidency was his destiny, and no one was going to change that fact, democrats or republicans.

CHAPTER 27

THE FINAL INNING

I had another dream that we all gathered in a stadium and compared notes in this competitive game of bullying. The similarities were quite astonishing: no matter how we look, walk, or talk, the bullies chose us because of the smell that they feared in the air. We were bound for greatness because of destiny. The charismatic embrace of future strongholds lead the way through the dark clouds into the sparkling sunlight each day we awake. I abruptly disturbed the game and got the microphone and loudly told the superstars, "We are a part of the Fatigue League." Our challengers, the bullies and their bystanders, were classified as the "Minor League." The children that go to school and harm no one are a part of the "Major League." In all schools, there are students that have no toleration for behavior issues and achieve academic success. For that reason alone, they are in a class all by themselves, the Major League. So, they are in the stands watching the game during the final inning, awaiting the winner. The Fatigue League takes the field and shakes hands and says, "Game on." Our coach, Jesus, gathers the team and gives us the game plan. In order to win the game, there are several innings that you must complete.

Inning number one: recognize who you are. You need to know your strengths and weaknesses. I was charismatic and a people-person. Although my bullies hated me, I was loved by many. The Lord made me aware that I wasn't perfect. I was born with two black eyes and looked like a raccoon. I later learned to accept it. My inner beauty outshined my lack of physical beauty. I later blossomed into who God wanted me to be, a self-confident, beautiful, brown-eyed woman. Every where I go now in life, older and younger people acknowledge that I have some beautiful eyes. The very thing I feared in my younger days has been a turning point in my latter days. It gave my bullies ground to walk on and made me stronger as a person. Never be ashamed of who you are, and recognize that the reason you are imperfect is because, if he made you perfect, then there will be no foundation for you to build upon. Self-confidence is a growing process that should be enhanced daily. You should look in the mirror every day and ask yourself, "What must I improve today?" Now, twenty years later, I believe that I am one of the prettiest girls God created. It took me years to build the foundation on rock, and don't think anyone can tear me down at his or her leisure. My team members were inspired by my story as they were waiting patiently to finish their storylines.

Inning number two: you must face your fears. Facing your fears reminds you that one day you will be noticed as the outcast. It will allow you to ride the school bus even though your heart desires for your parents to take you to school. Facing your fears will be an ultimate test to face your bullies head on, showing your willpower and strength. Over time, you will build self-humility. If your bullies know that you are avoiding them at all costs, then this will make your challenge harder to overcome. Bullies take notes as well, and if you are avoiding them, you have given them a lot of power because they know their words or actions are deteriorating you emotionally. Your school days will become nightmares, and you will be daydreaming about their next attack. The bullied child will be emotionally distressed from school, and the focus will not be on good grades. Facing your fears not only demonstrates strength but a need to be in control of your own destiny.

Facing your fears will assist you in the recovery process from name calling, physical threats, and being portrayed as the weakest link. You are the weakest link if you are not standing up for yourself.

Facing your fears allows you to approach your bullies and say, "I dare you to try and throw me in a garbage can or flush my head down a toilet bowl." Tell your bullies that you will hurt them each time they taunt you with threats. Show your courage by facing your fears head on. You show resilience in a way that's indescribable. You face challenges better if you don't run from the fears and show that you have power, self-esteem, and dignity. In this process, you build more of a solid platform that other students will follow.

When a bully throws a stone, you will administer the pain better and handle it proactively. If you study it, each situation that's thrown at you prepares you for a far better grade for the next step of success.

Facing your fears over time will help you with the embarrassment shoved at you in front of your peers. You will look at them dead in the eyes and say, "I was born to win this fight, but you will always be on defense and my offense will win this victory." With my self-motivation, I will come out well accomplished.

Tina the Termite faced her fears without shedding any tears. It showed my humility, character, and perseverance. With all the battles fought to weaken my character, shedding no tears made my victory even more successful. I didn't allow my bullies to see me teary eyed because they would have seen me at an emotionally weakened stage of the fight. When they walked by and hit me, I fought back with pride. Determination was a key factor in the battle against my bullies. I didn't want them to win. Each day I went to school, the verbal message conveyed was that each time you call me a name I will call your momma a bad name. The fights were ugly. They figured if they called me a name, I would cry and break down in front of the crowd. One day, bullies kept calling me ugly, and I told them that their momma was ugly and so were they.

Inning number three: fight your battle and own your battleground. If a bully pushes and shoves you around, physically fight back. Don't be afraid to give it all you got. It's okay if you don't win all your fights. You will lose some, but over time you will win with your self-confidence. The bullying battle will get more difficult if you don't fight back. I know some parents would wonder, "Why is she encouraging students to fight?" The short, simple answer would be, "It builds self-courage." On the contrary, if you don't fight back, then you will dream of the attacks and won't escape the nightmares when you close your eyes. Sleepless nights will become a syndrome that has no cure. The bullies will fearlessly spot your weaknesses. As you continue to show signs of courage, then it will only be a verbal battle versus a physical battle.

Inning number four: determination sets the pathway for destiny. If you have a determined mindset going into school every day, nothing should get in the way of your dream. Each bullied child should be determined to undermine the bullies' messages. The message is to destroy and degrade your self-image. You can undermine their message by doing your daily self-evaluation, build your self-respect, and love yourself. There should be never be a moment that you give your enemy any leverage over you. If they call you names, walk away with a smile. You can't stop them from calling you names, but if they physically touch you, then be determined to show that you are fighter. Eventually, the ladder of success becomes easier to climb. At the top of the ladder is your destiny. Ignore everyone in the way that seems to be a distraction because it's time to embrace destiny.

Inning number five: discover you. At this point in the game, you should have discovered yourself and know that you are a winner. This was a fight that I had to endure, and it made me realize that I can do anything in Christ who strengthens me. If I set my eye on becoming a singer, writer, dancer, actor, actress, golfer, comedian, swimmer, model, advocate for a cause, or president, I know that I can achieve my goal. Surround yourself with creativity and flee from negativity and your quality of life will improve significantly. Once you walk across the stage at graduation, it will hit you that the rest of your life belongs to you. I must discover my talents because that will be my guiding light.

Inning number six: turn pain into passion. During the long years of suffering from bullying, turn your pain into passion. Channel every thought about what the bullies said into a positive one. Find what makes you happy and focus on you. This will drive your passion for what you love to do. Whatever your talent is, try to excel and become the best you can be.

Inning number seven: passion fueled by purpose. You know how it feels to be bullied mercilessly, so if you notice another student experiencing your pain, step in and try to comfort someone else. Let them know that trouble doesn't last always. Share the details of how you are overcoming the fears and dealing with being an outcast. Everyone has a purpose in life, and once you discover your place, this will be the fuel that lights the fire.

Inning number eight: faith's reward. If you have faith in your higher power, he will not let you down. God will conquer your world and shield you with his love. You are going through the trial for a reason. We all have a season that we are tested. In order to receive your reward at the finish line, you must not give up along the way. He said your reward is life. Never choose to commit suicide under any circumstances. The enemy has won if you choose suicide. Be determined to earn your Survivor of the Years award.

Inning number nine, the final inning: platform for perseverance. After you have accomplished winning the first eight innings, number nine is where you set the stage for the rest of your life. When you look back over your life, the bullies said over and over again that you would never be anything. Now, this is the time you lay the groundwork for success because failure is not an option. You strive for excellence and perfection in everything that you do in life. Setting the platform for perseverance, your standards are high in order to conquer this fight. Allowing your bullies to underestimate you and create self-doubt weakens your base. That base starts with you. Other bullied children will want to be like you because you persevered against the fight and it made you a stronger person. This will be the toughest battle in every bullied child's life. If you leave school mad every day, disliking school, wanting to throw up, becoming anti-social at home, and closing yourself in your room, then you haven't completed your mental homework. If someone spends his or her time and energy to bring you down, then there is something about you that he or she envies. Don't ask yourself, "What is wrong with me?" Ask yourself, "What am I doing right?"! You are bound to become a superstar, but let no one sabotage your platform for perseverance because you were born to win.

CHAPTER 28
THE VICTORY

The final inning is almost over, and so far, the Fatigue League's score is higher than the Minor League's. Tina the Termite took base again, and she wanted to emphasize the importance of her story for today's generation. All the other team members of the Fatigue League wanted to highlight part of their stories, and some were too embarrassed to share their bullying stories because of their bullied names.

She endured so much pain over her ten-year struggle with bullies but persevered through it all. They hit her on the head with bats and poles and blacked her eye, but still she went to school the next day. She loved going to school and didn't care that her eye was swollen and black. While all the students pointed at her, laughing and making fun of her, she felt good on the inside. In between classes every day, she had to face bullies at her locker singing a song about her real name: "*T* is for Termite, *I* is for In the face, *N* is for Naturally ugly, *A* is for All the time, Tina the Termite." It was embarrassing, but she faced her fears. Not once did she have anxiety, close herself in her room at home, hate going to school, attempt suicide, or experience anti-social behavior. She didn't let the bullies define her or change her personality. However, it did make her stronger and stronger as a person. The first year that the bullying began, she failed reading and had to go to summer school because she was distracted by her rats. After the fact, she was an honor roll student every year and achieved personal and academic success.

Susie the Simple took base and said, "I was beaten badly by students and teachers, but I didn't let them win, and it took some time to achieve my nine-inning goal, but now I stand before you today as self-confident, accomplished, and the 'humble one.'" The devil meant it for bad, but God meant it for good. Let your voice be heard and the record-sale success be documented and the bullies words will be meaningless.

Michelle the Mudturtle also took base, and others were inspired by her story. "I want the world to know that I have received many awards in life and have been recognized as a star on the Hollywood Walk of Fame, but the award personally fulfilling to me is the Survivor of the Years award. It was an honor to have won such a tough race, but I dedicate the award to my bullies for molding my success. I have to admit, the taunts stayed with me in my thirties, but I have moved right along with destiny as an award-winning actress."

The stadium is full of excitement and the bases are loaded with Tina the Termite, Susie the Simple, and Michelle the Mudturtle. We were all wondering who would take the plate and hit the homerun for our team. As the team debated who would go next, the crowd enthusiastically cheered on Michael Phelps.

As he approached base, he looked up at his fans and gracefully thanked the Minor League for making the game competitive. He said, "Without you, there would be no game." Although people doubted me, I had confidence in myself, which is the most important step in my victory. I am the world's best Olympian because I was born to be the best. Never give up on the game because if you stay focused on yourself, in the end you will have claimed the victory. The Minor League can't win unless you give them the power. Take charge of your battlefield and claim what's yours. We are the Fatigue League because we were chosen to be a part of this league. I didn't realize it at first, but superstar power, charisma, and willpower to succeed define this league, and I am honored to be a part of such a team.

"Tina the Termite mentioned that we would like to pay tribute to some team members that struck out of the game during the second inning and didn't face their fears. These team members were charismatic and gifted, but instead of facing their fears, suicide became their choice. Phoebe Prince, Megan Meier, Kristina Calco, April Himes, Jared High, Desire Dryer, Austin Murphy, and Cassie Gielecki were all destined to walk the red carpet someday but were defeated by the Minor League."

"Now, back to the game," Tina the Termite told the crowd of fans. "There's a difference between being teased and being a target of bullies. Many students play around with each other, laugh, and call each other names out of fun. Some get teased simply because they have stolen a boyfriend or girlfriend from another. But there are others that are a target every day, every week, and every month. There is something mysterious about someone being the focus of another's attention that much. That is the first sign that your stardom has begun to blossom and others can smell your aroma in the air. As you continue to grow in age, the spotlight and invisible cameras will be on you. It will become more noticeable that you are a superstar that was born to lead, whether it is at school, church, a community, or at shows and events in your city.

"In the end, we have all learned that the only way you will win this game is to supersede your challengers' score in each inning." The superstars have exceeded the expectations of the master's plan and therefore have been crowned with victory. The race has now built an infrastructure that needs minor construction only because the platform needs strengthened annually.

"There are always things about us that we can change throughout our lives for our betterment and advancement, not because bullies implied it is so. It is because we grow as the seasons change."

Bullying has occurred for centuries, and they speculate why, but the real doctor, God, has diagnosed many superstars with bull fever and the end results are that there is no cure for the disease. He did inform all the superstars that in order for the disease not to become more contagious or get worst that they will need to take their medicine every day for the rest of their lives. Although you will continue to get poked with the deadly needle, the pain will not last now that you know the cause and continue to take your prescribed medicines.

"Many are called All Stars, 'teased,' but only a few are chosen as Superstars, 'targets.' If you are chosen, there is an advantage in your favor and don't drink your bullies' flavor and give into the temptations of suicide because the law requires you to fulfill a life of a higher calling."

POEM DEDICATED TO BULLIED CHILDREN:
BULL FEVER

As I walk with honor
Bullies chose me as a donor
My temperature rises
As it reaches an all time high
They poked me,
With a deadly needle
The tip was infected
With a serious disease.

Temporarily my mind
Went into a blackout
From the unexpectancy
Of the damage to the brain

When awakened,
Suddenly I realized,
The cause was unknown
But the affect was failure
Fever allowed my body
To fight off the abnormal infection.

Couple days passed by,
I reached toward the sky
Maybe there's a star
To shed some light
On an illness my body seems to fight

There's a reason my name
Is on the bullies donor's list of fame
The Agencies couldn't figure it out,
The world remained clueless,
Puzzled by man,
It was answered from above.

I am bullied for a reason,
This is my season
There's will inside of me
That shines so bright
Make it obvious I can fight
Off any infection that comes my way.

I wear the daily armour
Of my higher power,
Body needed a shower,
To cleanse the germs
From my evil bullies

After the fact, the needle shots,
Short term pain didn't phase me,
As I realized just as the animal, "Bull"
Is allergic to the color "Red"

The angel from above
Showed me why I was diagnosed
With "Bullied fever",
Because I was the future "Star"
Live on the "Red" Carpet.

ACKNOWLEDGMENTS

I would like to start first by saying thanks to my parents, who provided wisdom and knowledge throughout my journey. You have made my life worth living and provided that stable home environment for all seven of your kids. Although I loved going to school each and every day, the most fulfilling moments of my life were when I came home from school. We had a vital bond that helps strengthen a child's foundation, values, beliefs, and sense of purpose in life. You taught us the true meaning of the word *love* and encouraged us to be the best we can be. One of your favorite quotes was to "never give up on life." I live by this motto daily because I always find a reason to keep on going and to continue to search for life's destiny. I am really grateful to you because y'all are the best parents a child could ask for. Special thanks for bringing us up in the Pentecostal church because it taught me true holiness. Even when you both were not in regular attendance, you motivated me to continue my journey through Covington Church of God in Christ. I was the only child still going on a regular basis with Grandmother. Both sets of my grandparents continuously preached love, love, love. If you have love in your heart, you will find reasons not to talk about an individual. If you don't have anything positive to say, remain speechless. For that I say thanks, because it has molded my beauty inside and out.

To my siblings, thanks for believing in me and keeping the faith. When I first discovered the calling to write, you all doubted me at first, but you stuck by me through thick and thin. It takes a lot of support to write a book, and it has been a challenge that I was willing to face. If I needed to ask a question or had a concern throughout the process, the phone didn't go unanswered; the ear remained attentive to my needs and aspirations. For that, I owe you sincere gratitude.

Huge thanks to my brother, Richard. You were there by my side through the journey of the "Bullied Child." When the bullies called me names, hit me on the head with poles, attacked me from behind, or tried to trip me with their feet, you came out of nowhere to help fight my battles. There were times that I didn't think I could do it alone, and you made a way out of darkness. You were one of my inspirations and I knew you were not only my brother, but a friend to the end. During my freshman year in college, you were late for your classes to come check on your little sister. You introduced yourself to everyone, acknowledging that I was your sister and stated that, "If anyone seeks to harm her, they will have to answer to me." This really spoke high volumes of the brother/sister bond that we shared. I love you so much!

I owe a huge amount of devotion and appreciation to my wonderful husband. Without you, the "Aftermath" of twenty years later would be missing a crucial piece to its lengthy puzzle. I found peace and happiness during my senior year in college. It was a blessing to have worked three days at Louisiana Pacific. I was at the right place at the right time or else I would probably still be on my soul mate journey. I am thankful for another bond we share, our beautiful daughter, Avriss. The both of you make my world complete.

Last but not least, I would like to shine some light on the institutions that help pave the way for my academic success: Covington High School, Rust College, and UNCF. I want to thank you all for allowing me to become a recipient from 1997 to 2001. Without your support, I couldn't afford to walk on the campus of one of the most recognized historically black colleges in the United States. President David Beckley and the Rust College staff, I want to personally thank you for such wonderful college years, and lastly, graduating with a Bachelor's degree, a dream to some but reality to many. This was one of the proudest moments in my life. Never in a million years would one imagine notes that are written in your senior high school book to come true. I wrote, "I would like to graduate from college with an accounting degree." Thank you so much. I pray for CHS, UNCF, and Rust College's continued success!